JCSS Study No. 5

THE AMERICAN APPROACH TO SUPERPOWER COLLABORATION IN THE MIDDLE EAST, 1973-1986

Abraham Ben-Zvi

WESTVIEW PRESS
Boulder, Colorado

WESTVIEW PRESS
Frederick A. Praeger, Publisher
5500 Central Avenue
Boulder, Colorado 80301

JCSS Studies
are published for the Jaffee Center
for Strategic Studies
by
The Jerusalem Post
POB 81, Jerusalem 91000, Israel
and
Westview Press
Boulder, Colorado 80301, Frederick A. Praeger, Publisher

Printed in Israel at the Jerusalem Post Press

ISBN 0-8133-0461-x
LC 86-40371

Contents

Acknowledgments

I wish to thank Alexander L. George, Aharon Klieman, Aharon Yariv, Tamar Herman, Mark Heller, Joseph Alpher, Shai Feldman and Ariel Levite for their thoughtful suggestions and comments on earlier drafts of this work. I am also indebted to Joseph Alpher for his meticulous, thoroughly professional and insightful editing work.

Summary

In recent years, the specific role of the superpowers in a comprehensive Middle East settlement has become the subject of incessant scholarly and journalistic debate. In order to better elucidate this subject and help eliminate at least some of the simplistic dichotomies and generalizations which abound in the literature, this work develops a cognitive framework for outlining the parameters of the American search for a superpower settlement in the area since the Yom Kippur War of October 1973. Specifically, two broad types of basic foreign policy orientations, from which were derived incompatible peace strategies in the Arab-Israeli sphere, are distinguished: (a) the bipolar-confrontational conception, which is divided into pure and mitigated variants; and (b) the multipolar-accommodative conception.

Using this typology as an analytical tool, the work examines American peacemaking diplomacy as it has unfolded since 1973. Kissinger's exclusionist approach was based on a mitigated form of the bipolar-confrontational orientation; it delimited and constrained the scope of superpower collaboration. In contrast, Carter's collaborative posture was derived from his multipolar-accommodative outlook, and attempted to involve the Soviet Union in *all* phases of the peacemaking effort.

Lessons drawn from the failure of Carter's effort to elicit Soviet cooperation in jointly shaping a settlement are conducive to framing a set of predictions regarding the feasibility and effectiveness of future collaborative strategies. Any renewed attempt to establish a superpower condominium in the region will have to meet two constraints: the first, a domestic constraint, requires that an adequate base of domestic support for the legitimacy of such a posture be established; the second, an external constraint, demands that a sufficient measure of international support for the legitimacy of the collaborative course be consolidated.

In view of widespread, on-going American domestic opposition to such a strategy, as well as the unwavering opposition of at least some of the local parties to a superpower solution (as demonstrated in the aftermath of the October 1, 1977 superpower communique on the Middle East), there is little immediate prospect for a short-term or middle-term American strategy of superpower condominium.

Chapter 1. American Images of the International System: A Theoretical Framework

In recent years, the specific role of the superpowers in a comprehensive Middle East settlement has become the subject of incessant and heated debate among scholarly and journalistic circles. Yet this preoccupation with the American-Soviet dyad as the key to a regional accommodation has not precipitated any systematic survey of the major variables and constraints which might determine the efficacy of pressures, exerted jointly by the superpowers, and designed to influence client behavior.

The following analysis will attempt to bridge this conceptual and empirical lacuna by integrating a number of cognitive categories and typologies into an essentially historical context. Specifically, divergent American preconceptions of the Soviet Union, which unfolded during the period following the Yom Kippur War of October 1973, are depicted as independent variables which defined the parameters of the American interest in superpower collaboration as it sought to terminate or at least moderate the protracted Arab-Israeli conflict.

In seeking to elucidate the patterns by which Washington's decisionmakers approached both their domestic and external environments, we may surmise that "there exist for presidential administrations certain 'strategic' or 'geopolitical' codes, assumptions about American interests in the world, potential threats to them, and feasible responses, that tend to be formed either before or just after an administration takes office."[1]

This reliance on an essentially cognitive framework by no means implies that the linkage between cognition and decision is necessarily linear, or that images and belief systems always comprise a set of mathematical algorithms that the actor applies mechanically during the decisionmaking process.[2] To safeguard against this kind of error, we shall integrate into the analysis such antecedent factors as systemic, situational, organizational and role variables, which occasionally (as in the inception of the Rogers Plan) played a major role in the shaping of American peace strategies in the Middle East. As George observes, this cluster of non-cognitive categories certainly may contribute to explaining the emergence of

3

a particular decision or policy initiative; indeed, in certain settings it may dwarf the perceptual variables in determining the decision. [3] Thus, while employing cognitive categories and notions as its principal explanatory tool, our examination of the divergent American images of the world and the region will treat the factors comprising the psychological environment of foreign policy elites not as unmitigated determinants of policy prescription, but rather as a prism through which decisionmakers may orient themselves to the environment. [4]

In applying a set of cognitive premises to the study of conflict resolution in the Arab-Israeli sphere, it is also assumed that pre-existing images of the world, though usually changing only marginally during the course of a specific crisis or decision episode, are not fixed and stable concepts, totally immune to modification. Rather, they are dynamic notions which may ultimately undergo considerable adjustment as a result of cumulative learning experiences or the impact of domestic or environmental constraints. Thus the architects of American diplomacy, while seeking to maintain cognitive consistency and to fit incoming information into their preconceived beliefs and expectations, could not remain totally oblivious over time to major international developments that exposed serious gaps between the "operational environment" and their own "psychological environment." [5] Indeed, as we shall soon witness in typologizing the predominant American beliefs concerning the global international system during most of the 1970s, some pre-existing images of the Soviets' operational code and long-range objectives eventually receded into the background: they were replaced by a cluster of incompatible "immediate images," delineated in accordance with the specific patterns of interaction which developed on the global level. [6] With time, the complex of views comprising these "immediate images" was at least partially integrated into the actors' original belief systems, leading them to modify various tenets of their foreign policy orientations. Specifically, the encounter with a recalcitrant reality led both presidents Carter and Reagan to deviate significantly from some of their preliminary visions of the world, and ultimately to embark on policy initiatives which were clearly at variance with their original cognitive maps.

Thus the Carter foreign policy elite's encounter with the "operational environment" forced it to reconsider its global priorities and ultimately to focus on the very East-West rivalries which it had perceived initially as less pressing than the need to address the economic and social plight of the Third World. In the case of the Reagan entourage, the learning experience accumulated during its first term in office precipitated a significant moderation of its initial intensely confrontational orientation toward Moscow.

On the regional level, the Carter administration eventually abandoned its collaborative strategy of negotiating comprehensive peace at Geneva and embarked instead on an exclusionist posture, which culminated in the Camp David accords. In contrast, the Reagan policy elite gradually moved from the extreme of unilateralism (as manifested in the Reagan Peace Plan of September 1, 1982) to a more ambivalent strategy, which incorporated certain collaborative elements regarding the Soviet role in the peacemaking process. This was demonstrated in 1985 by Washington's qualified readiness to involve Moscow in certain phases of the multilateral drive which American diplomacy hoped to set in motion in 1986.

Finally, in examining the predominant patterns of perception which precipitated such peacemaking initiatives as the Geneva peace conference in the wake of the Yom Kippur War or the joint superpower statement on the Middle East of October 1, 1977, our analysis will concentrate on the different American visions of the Soviet role in the diplomatic process. For, while the Soviet approach toward a comprehensive settlement fluctuated occasionally during this period in nuance and emphasis, it is on the American side that one encounters vacillation, inconsistency and sharp breaks with past strategies and predilections.

During the period which followed the 1967 war, the Soviet position on the Arab-Israeli conflict consistently incorporated the following elements:

> In the first place..., all territories occupied by Israel since 1967 — the Golan Heights, the West Bank of the Jordan River, the Gaza Strip and the Lebanese lands — must be returned to the Arabs. Second, the right of the Arab people of Palestine to self-determination and to the creation of their own independent state on the Palestinian lands...must be ensured....Third, the eastern part of Jerusalem...must be returned to the Arabs and become an inseparable part of the Palestinian state....Fourth, the right of all states of the area must be ensured to safe and independent existence.... Fifth, an end must be put to the state of war, and peace must be

5

established between the Arab states and Israel....Sixth, international guarantees of settlement must be drawn up...by the permanent members of the UN Security Council.

This plan was to be endorsed by an international conference, with the participation of the superpowers and "all the sides concerned."[7] Occasionally, as during the Nixon-Brezhnev summit of June 1973, the Soviet Union sought to persuade the US to accept most of these principles as an impetus for rapid implementation of its vision of a superpower condominium. American leaders, however, strongly resisted pressures for an imposed settlement "that would heavily favor the Arabs."[8]

In contrast to the fixed parameters of the Soviet posture, American peacemaking strategies in the Arab-Israeli sphere after 1973 reflected widely divergent foreign policy orientations.

They shifted from the pole of unilateralism (predicated upon a confrontational, intensely bipolar vision of the international system), to the extreme of collaboration (based on an essentially accommodative view of the global environment). The fact that each paradigm was applied to the extreme and was implemented ad absurdum, contributed to its eventual replacement by an antithetical category."

Notwithstanding such fundamental differences, all peace strategies pursued by the US since 1973 shared one premise, namely, the desire to mitigate the Arab-Israeli predicament. Fearing that continued tension and animosity along the Arab-Israeli front could well involve the superpowers in an acutely dangerous confrontation, *all* US administrations sought to defuse the conflict or at least to control the risks of escalation. Thus President Nixon, from his first days in the White House, repeatedly alluded to what was to become a major tenet in American thinking and behavior during the entire period under discussion — the highly menacing vision of a regional conflict escalating into a direct superpower conflagration:

> I believe we need new initiatives and new leadership on the part of the United States in order to cool off the situation in the Mideast. I consider it a powder keg, very explosive. It needs to be defused. I am open to any suggestions that may cool it off and reduce the possibility of another explosion, because the next explosion in the Mideast, I think, could involve very well a confrontation between the nuclear powers, which we want to avoid.[10]

In an effort to convert these seemingly contradictory policies into a more coherent pattern, our analysis will first present a typology of American visions of the world and of the bounds of national security within which certain images of the Soviet Union and its role in a Middle East settlement were delineated. Then, in chapters 2 and 3, the categories and distinctions comprising this cognitive typology will be applied to the analysis of two case studies — Secretary Kissinger's mediation effort during the period following the Yom Kippur War, and President Carter's diplomatic drive, which culminated on October 1, 1977, to engage the Soviets in the search for regional accommodation. In addition, the views and actions of other foreign policy elites (such as the Reagan entourage) which did not trigger any major superpower initiative in the region, will be explained in terms of the conceptual notions and premises developed earlier. It is hoped that by linking these behavioral patterns to cognitive predispositions, a clearer view regarding the parameters and prospects of future peacemaking efforts will emerge.

The literature surveying the conceptual premises of crisis decisionmaking in American foreign policy is permeated with dichotomous concepts and interpretations. Concentrating on several emotion-laden issues during the post-World War II era, such as the origins of the Cold War and the roots of American intervention in Vietnam, a large number of scholars have produced highly polemical literature on the subject. In many of these analyses the tendency has been to view American diplomacy as either "realistic and self-interested to the point of rapacious," or as "naive, overly idealistic, and moralistic."[11]

Alongside such one-dimensional explanations, another group of scholars has sought a more integrated interpretation of the dominant orientations in American foreign policy. An illustration of this interdisciplinary effort to shed light on the dynamics of decisionmaking processes in crisis situations is Snyder and Diesing's comprehensive study, *Conflict Among Nations*.[12] The work argues that US foreign policy is seldom shaped by a single factor or trend. Rather, it has been the outcome of constant competition between two distinctive types of political actors who differ widely in their basic perceptions of world politics. Snyder and Diesing label these divergent types "hard-liner" and "soft-liner" decisionmakers. According to their analysis, the hard-liner perceives relations among nations as fundamentally conflictual:

"nations, particularly adversary nations, are engaged in a virtually Hobbesian pursuit of power." Consequently, he is acutely sensitive to "power-strategic considerations, to the potential aggressiveness of other states, and to the need to preserve or improve the power and security position of his own state." He is committed to the notion that the opponent is pursuing virtually unlimited expansionist objectives, and can only be contained through unadulterated coercion. Thus he usually advocates utmost firmness and irreconcilability in crisis situations as the optimal way of deterring and restraining adversary statesmen.[13]

By comparison, the soft-liner's overall perspective toward international affairs stresses harmony rather than conflict. Perceiving the opponent's long-range objectives as limited and specific, he believes that conciliatory gestures are likely "to give rise to mutual efforts to compromise," whereas harsh, coercive measures can only elicit retaliatory, recalcitrant behavior on the part of the adversary. The soft-liner is convinced that the opposing camp always comprises a heterogeneous entity; hence he is confident that his preferred strategy of conciliation will strengthen the moderate faction in the rival state and pave the way toward accommodation. Thus the moderate decisionmaker differs sharply from the hard-liner, whose intransigent behavior in crisis situations derives from the belief that conflict is perpetual and animosities permanent.[14]

Synder and Diesing's analysis of the differences between hard-liners and soft-liners in terms of the content of certain incompatible cognitive maps is accompanied by a structural distinction between the rational and irrational bargainer. They maintain that as a given crisis situation unfolds, the rational bargainer may react increasingly to the immediate conflict pattern and less to his basic perceptions, which gradually recede into the background. In such situations, actual behavior may therefore be decoupled from preexisting images of the opponent's operational code and long-range objectives. The behavior of the irrational bargainer, on the other hand, is always dominated by a rigid belief system.[15] Whereas the rational bargainer "is not one who 'knows' at the start of a crisis what the situation is, what the relative interests, power relations, and the main alternatives are," the irrational bargainer is predisposed to diagnose and interpret the situation solely by means of his initial belief system. "Knowing" in advance what the opponents' fundamental characteristics and ultimate aims are, the irrational bargainer remains irreconcilably committed to his chosen strategy through all diversions and difficulties.[16]

Snyder and Diesing succeeded in developing a coherent conceptual framework, whose categories and distinctions help to replace some of the crude interpretations which abound in the literature surveying American diplomatic history. However, for all this theoretical innovativeness, there still remains a question as to the precise roots of both the recalcitrant and the conciliatory patterns of behavior in specific conflict situations. In other words, while the gap between these divergent types of decisionmakers is a recurrent characteristic of many a crisis, it is not entirely clear where the divisions originate. Do they indeed derive from general, incompatible attitudes to human nature and the essence of social life, or from more specific perceptions of the contemporary international system? Furthermore, although Snyder and Diesing refer briefly and intermittently to the category of the middle-line bargainer, who "combines hard and soft features in varying degrees and may seem hard in one context and soft in another,"[17] their work focuses largely on two dichotomous ideal types. Preoccupied as they are with "the two extremes of belligerence and cooperation, of coercion and accommodation," they are bound to minimize or obfuscate the more subtle and unobtrusive distinctions between the various sub-types of hard-line or soft-line behavior. Yet it is precisely the shades and nuances which are of crucial importance in determining the specific parameters within which certain peacemaking initiatives in the Arab-Israeli arena were shaped.

In order to better elucidate this question and further differentiate the factors determining intransigent as opposed to moderate attitudes in decision episodes, this analysis concentrates on the patterns by which the concept of "national security" was defined by several high-ranking American decisionmakers during the period under consideration. It is argued that while a number of policymakers who advocated incompatible policies did share some components of their belief systems, they nonetheless differed widely in their respective definitions of the bounds of American national interests.

The most pervasive of these different conceptions of US vital interests which have occasioned divergent policy recommendations may be termed: 1) the bipolar-confrontational conception, which in turn is divided into two sub-types — the pure type and the mitigated or moderate variant; and 2) the multipolar-accommodative conception. It is to the analysis of these two divergent conceptions, and their nuanced variations, that we now turn.

Chapter 2.
The Bipolar-Confrontational Conception

Reagan and the Pure Type: Presentation

The bipolar-confrontational category approximates, in its various manifestations, what Holsti labels "Cold War Internationalism," what Yergin terms "The Riga axioms," what Dallin and Lapidus define as an "essentialist" approach and what Schneider calls "conservative internationalism."[1] It is predicated upon an all-inclusive definition of the parameters of American national security. The words of James Forrestal captured its essence in arguing that "Our national security can only be assured on a very broad and compehensive front."[2]

Statesmen and diplomats of this category are irrevocably committed to the notion that all points on the global map are equally close, that every crisis is of equal importance, and that a tight linkage exists among a multitude of political, economic and military factors operating in the international system.[3] They are predisposed to couple limited conflicts with the global balance of power, and thus to broaden or "delocalize" their scope and parameters:[4]

> They [the Cold War Internationalists] perceive a conflictual world in which the primary cleavages are those dividing the East and the West, and in which most, if not all the salient issues and conflicts, are closely linked to each other and to that fault line. As a result of such tight lines, disturbances in one region will reverberate throughout the international system.[5]

Convinced that events halfway around the globe have an automatic, direct impact on America's core interests, confrontational decisionmakers tend to view *any* adverse turn of events anywhere as directly endangering the United States. Consequently, they translate desirable foreign policy goals into issues of national survival, and the range of threats becomes limitless. Because they believe that international crises are seldom local, isolated phenomena, but rather are elements within the worldwide communist effort to disrupt the global balance of power and thereby to threaten the security of the US, they underscore the need to stand firm and resist *any* attempt at encroachment, whatever its origin or location.

The specific strategy derived from these premises may range from an effort at selective containment to an attempt to push a hostile and expansionist superpower back within its borders ("rollback"). However, all confrontational strategies of containment, whether by deterrence, coercion or rollback, perceive international politics as a bipolar, zero-sum game in which the Soviet Union is "the chief enemy of world order."[6] Depicted as an inherently evil and expansionist entity which is committed to a global messianic design to challenge the status quo and implement its "master plan for world domination," the Soviet adversary can therefore be restrained only by a demonstration of American resoluteness. With a confrontational, intensely bipolar view of this sort, any effort to reach lasting, comprehensive agreements (let alone to pursue a policy of condominium, which implies some degree of joint control) becomes irrelevant, even dangerous. For the Cold War confrontation is considered preordained in the revolutionary and predatory character of the Soviet Union.[7]

This sweeping insistence on the broadest parameters of national security and on the adversary's long-term, fixed objectives, precludes any attempt to analyze a local crisis on its own merits. The local event is perceived as but one facet of a larger phenomenon, whose significance lies beyond the regional boundaries within which it unfolds. It is stripped, a priori, of whatever particular characteristics it may have possessed, and is thus elevated to the superpower level:

> The United States on the whole has tended...to underrecognize the independent roles and initiatives of third world countries and third parties....Paradoxically, the United States, with an ideology championing pluralism and pragmatism in the conduct of foreign relations, has tended in recent decades to view the world in excessively oversimplified terms — all other realities are subordinated to a conflict between a "Free World" and a "Communist World," headed respectively by the United States and the Soviet Union.[8]

Lastly, the bipolar-confrontational conception focuses its attention not on what the Soviet Union does, but on what it is believed to be. Highly determinist in approach, this perspective sees little prospect for transforming a tight bipolar- confrontational system into a more accommodative world order. Rather, it is committed to a dichotomous vision of the world, and to an ultra-hard image of the Soviet opponent. It predicates its strategy on the premises of deterrence and coercion — whether by confrontation, challenge, or hostility, albeit short of war. But it remains unwavering in its opposition to any form of accommodation — whether by coexistence, adaptation, or cooperation.[9]

Proceeding from the realm of the philosophical to the level of the operational, it appears that the initial background images of the world held by President Reagan and some of his associates and advisers, including Jean Kirkpatriek, William P. Clark, Richard Perle, Richard Allen and Richard Pipes, approximated the pure type of the bipolar-confrontational category.[10] Motivated by a pervasive, highly-threatening perception of the Soviet Union as an inherently aggressive entity "engaged in an unprecedented campaign of expansion," these members of Reagan's foreign policy elite were convinced that Soviet promotion of violence as the instrument of change constituted "the greatest danger to world peace."[11] As President Reagan pointed out in a *Time* interview in February 1981: "I know of no leader of the Soviet Union...that has not more than once repeated...[his] determination that [his] goal must be the promotion of world communism and a one-world socialist or communist state...."[12] The memoirs of Alexander Haig cast a similar light on the administration's early unmitigated bipolar perspective: "Clearly, the Soviet Union..., because it insists upon the struggle of opposites as a matter of dogma, is and must remain the first concern of any US Administration... [the Soviets] and their surrogates chose the ground for revolution with bravado, but if no lines were drawn, how could they know whether they had gone too far?"[13]

As these statements clearly indicate, the conceptual point of departure of the Reagan foreign and defense policy elite in approaching the external environment was a dichotomous view of the world which portrayed the Soviet Union as "the last great predatory empire on earth,"[14] one that "involves ideological, economic, and military challenges to Western ideals, to Western political and economic systems, and to Western security." Considering the extent of the Soviet menace, the critical factor in curbing Soviet military power was "not what we do now but whether we are prepared to be firm and principled during the next decade."[15] Committed to a bipolar-confrontational definition of a tight linkage between seemingly diverse crises and areas, and to a broad, undifferentiated and indiscriminate definition of the bounds of American national security, the Reagan entourage was predisposed to place the subject of Soviet expansion in third areas at the very center of American-Soviet relations, and thus to view Third World problems solely within the context of Soviet-American rivalry. In the words of Secretary of State Haig: "When the Soviet Union exploits local conditions for its own strategic aims, the problem is no longer local but a strategic threat to our own survival. We cannot ignore this threat."[16]

Reacting to this vision of mounting threat, the Reagan administration articulated a philosophy "that gave promise of greater military strength, more aggressive diplomacy, and more active ideological and economic competition."[17] The Reagan elite emphasized deterrence and coercion rather than negotiation (at least until it had restored a global balance of power sufficient to convince the Soviet leadership that aggrandizement would not pay) as the most appropriate means to combat Soviet encroachment in the wake of the invasion of Afghanistan. In the Middle East, this precipitated an exclusionist strategy which assigned priority to the task of forging a regional security framework over any other traditional objective, including that of comprehensively mitigating the Arab-Israeli dispute. Indeed, Reagan's preoccupation with the need to contain the Soviet Union and to strengthen its regional allies against further Soviet penetration, took precedence over his efforts to make peace in the Middle East. American interest in containment was therefore linked to its regional conflict management strategy: "When the United States regarded Soviet ambitions and intentions with unremitting hostility and expressed a strong interest in containing the Soviet Union, it pursued a policy of benign neglect towards the Arab-Israeli conflict."[18] As candidate Reagan pointed out in his August 15, 1979, article in *The Washington Star*: "Stripped of rhetoric, the paramount American interest in the Middle East is to prevent the region from falling under the domination of the Soviet Union."

More specifically, members of the Reagan foreign policy machine initially assumed that only when the danger of continued Soviet encroachment had receded, would the local states, "feeling confident of US reliability and secure against the Soviet threat...be willing to take the necessary risks for peace."[19] Thus, during the winter and early spring of 1981, Secretary Haig repeatedly argued

14

that Riyadh's refusal to enter the peace process reflected the insecurities it felt — insecurities that had to be traced primarily to the Soviet Union or its regional proxies, and which were further compounded by lingering doubts about American credibility and reliability. If these insecurities could be effectively redressed, Haig predicted, the Saudi attitude toward the peace process might well change.

A new "strategic consensus" — a broad regional alliance against the Soviets — would, the new administration hoped, function as a bulwark against Soviet inroads into the region. Translated into concrete terms, this approach called for an accelerated search for "base facilities" in the area, and for the establishment of "divisions or units that could be projected...very rapidly" via those bases, to trouble spots. This new force alignment would act "as a deterrent to the Soviets for many more adventures coming in through Iran and Iraq and attempts to seize the oil fields," and would frustrate the Kremlin's ambitious drive "to displace the United States as the most influential foreign power between the Caspian Sea and the Indian Ocean."[20]

In many ways this was a throwback to President Eisenhower's bipolar-confrontational approach, which unfolded in the Middle East during the period 1953-1955. At that time the Eisenhower administration, motivated by the vision of a worldwide communist threat to the global balance of power, and alarmed by the rapid fall of all the East European states to Soviet domination after World War II, had embarked on a policy that sought to encircle the Soviet Union with states allied to and supported by the West. Determined to forge a security alliance among such regional powers as Turkey, Iraq and Pakistan, the administration — in accordance with the logic of the bipolar-confrontational paradigm which shaped its thinking and behavior — largely downgraded the objective of comprehensively resolving the Arab-Israeli predicament, as this would have entailed some form of superpower collaboration. And while sporadic and intermittent efforts were made from time to time (such as the Eric Johnston plan for sharing Jordan River waters), they fell considerably short of any multifaceted peace initiative.[21]

Thus in approaching the Middle East, the Reagan foreign policy elite's initial strategy was derived from its bipolar- confrontational orientation. It focused on the need to create a "strategic framework that recognizes and is responsive to the greater threat of Soviet expansionism,"[22] and a priori ruled out any attempt to solicit Soviet cooperation in defining the parameters of a regional settlement. Indeed, the administration's most comprehensive initiative to defuse the Arab-Israeli conflict during its first term — the Reagan Peace Plan of September 1, 1982 — was an exclusive American endeavor which was not preceded by any superpower discussions. Patterned on the premise of exclusiveness, it can be thought of as an effort to use the Lebanon War and some of its immediate, short-term ramifications as a springboard for promoting a wide range of strategic objectives at the expense of the Soviet Union and its local clients.[23]

In conclusion, a regional strategy on the Arab-Israeli front of the kind initially pursued by the Reagan entourage (and by the Eisenhower high policy elite three decades earlier) incorporates at least some of the premises of the pure type of the bipolar-confrontational approach. As such, it is by definition irrevocably opposed to the very notion of superpower cooperation, however delimited and constrained it might be. Reflecting the bipolar-confrontational predisposition "to isolate the Soviet Union, to deny it even symbolic recognition, parity, or legitimacy, and, in effect, to ostracize it in the international community," it was but the logical corollary of a basic propensity to refuse all negotiations with Moscow regarding the parameters of a settlement. As Dallin and Lapidus further observe,

> negotiations [were] at the opposite pole from political warfare on the spectrum of political relations. To refrain from negotiations also fitted the pragmatic argument that at some future point the United States would be in a stronger bargaining position, thanks to the military build-up the administration had launched and because of looming crises in the Soviet system.[24]

As already intimated, even strongly-held ideas and belief systems cannot always remain totally immune to the pressures of a dynamic world. In the case of the Reagan presidency, the preliminary pure bipolar-confrontational vision of the international system partially and incrementally receded into the background in the course of the president's first term in office. Instead, a cluster of more moderate components of the bipolar-confrontational orientation emerged toward the end of Reagan's first term, coexisting with the initial "essentialist" ingredients of the administration's world view. A detailed examination of the factors

16

which triggered this shift is beyond the scope of the present work. Clearly, however, they included a renewed sense of security derived from a strengthened military posture and the emerging prospects for developing advanced space warfare technology (thus enabling the US to enter negotiations from a position of strength), mounting domestic and external pressures (particularly from Europe) to negotiate with the Soviet Union over the entire range of arms control issues, and a desire to take advantage of new opportunities for improving the American bargaining position vis-à-vis the Soviet Union during the post-Brezhnev era. In any event, as the first term of the Reagan presidency approached its end, a more complex vision of a world comprising divergent elements replaced the preliminary dichotomous and combative view.[25]

Notwithstanding this willingness on the part of several members of Reagan's high policy elite to deviate from their initial pure bipolar-confrontational perspective and to accommodate themselves to the forces operating on the international scene, the newly-opened window of opportunity for managing adversary relations by means of negotiations, remained exceedingly narrow. For at least some of the administration's bipolar-confrontational notions and principles remained intact. Thus, as the Reagan-Gorbachev summit of November 1985 indicated, the administration, while prepared to incorporate the principle of negotiations at all levels into its world view, remained adamant in its opposition to any form of regional agreement that was patterned on the premises of superpower condominium and thus required the subordination of competitive elements to a collaborative regional design. As Secretary of State George Schultz stated in testimony before the Senate Foreign Relations Committee on January 31, 1985, in which he defined the scope of impending American-Soviet discussions, "We don't foresee any development that would lead us to want to come together with the Soviet Union for some sort of condominium about the Middle East."[26] And indeed, the first round of talks on the Middle East, held in Vienna on February 19-20, 1985, between Vladimir Polyakov (Head of the Near East Division of the Soviet Foreign Ministry) and Richard Murphy (Assistant Secretary of State for Near Eastern and South Asian Affairs), amounted to nothing more than "an exchange of views" that was designed, in President Reagan's words, "to make sure that there is no miscalculation that can cause a big problem."[27] Far from seeking to utilize the discussions to affect a comprehensive settlement of issues comprising the Arab-Israeli conflict, the administration — confronted with an irreconcilable Soviet posture on some of the parameters of a settlement in area of disputed high-interest asymmetry — perceived these superpower contacts as merely a crisis-prevention device, intended to regulate the parties' involvement in a highly volatile area, and thus to reduce the risks of dangerous confrontation and military clashes. A few days before the Vienna talks, State Department Spokesman Bernard Kalb refused even to label them as negotiations, maintaining that they would "not constitute negotiations nor are they intended to lead to broader negotiation....these talks are not the precursor of any agreements, nor are we going to seek any agreements in Vienna."[28]

The Vienna talks were construed as an integral part of the overall search to develop "patterns of restraint," which culminated in the November 1985 summit meeting between President Reagan and Soviet Premier Gorbachev. They endeavored to formulate norms, rules of engagement, or ad hoc ground rules which might reconcile continued support for local allies with the types of restraint needed to avoid escalation to undesirable levels of involvement and superpower conflict.[29] Similarly, statements made by such policymakers as Secretary Schultz in late May and early June 1985, in which the possibility of Soviet participation in a multilateral peacemaking effort on the Middle East was either given qualified support or alluded to in ambivalent terms, by no means indicated that the Reagan foreign policy apparatus had decided to set aside its initial desire to proceed unilaterally for the sake of eliciting Soviet cooperation in the quest for comprehensive peace (to be pursued under the auspices of an international conference). Rather, they reflected Washington's overriding wish to accommodate its policy with King Hussein's "desire to proceed somehow within the framework of broad international support."[30] Here, faced with Hussein's request for "an international umbrella" or "an international context" to legitimize any direct negotiating process between a joint Palestinian-Jordanian delegation and Israel, the Reagan entourage — without committing the US to any specific collaborative move vis-à-vis the Soviet Union — opted to obfuscate, at least temporarily, several components of its preliminary Middle East policy, and primarily its opposition to the very notion of an international conference as an appropriate mechanism for negotiating comprehensive peace. Still, the role assigned to the Soviet Union within such an international framework was essentially a cosmetic one. Thus it was expected that a Geneva style conference would merely provide a symbolic blessing for a diplomatic umbrella under which Jordanians, Palestinians and Israelis would negotiate peace, with the US as the sole mediator.

Finally, the discussion of the Middle East predicament, held in Geneva between President Reagan and Soviet party leader Gorbachev on November 20, 1985, fell considerably short of any attempt to coordinate strategies. Like the Vienna meeting of February 1985, it comprised merely an exchange of views. Indeed, a similar picture emerges from an analysis of the Soviet-American discussions on the Middle East held in Stockholm in June 1986.

In conclusion, while the Reagan team did eventually develop or sanction certain forms of minimalist superpower collaboration — mainly to prevent accidents and misunderstandings by establishing procedures for consultation — these isolated islands of cooperation within an otherwise highly conflictual setting fell considerably short of the concept of a superpower condominium, which entails "a comprehensive, harmonious and collusive definition of interests, geared toward jointly imposing on weaker states terms for conflict resolution that the superpowers have worked out on their own."[31] Nor did these delimited areas of cooperation even approximate less comprehensive definitions of a condominium which refer to "some degree of joint control" between the superpowers.[32]

The Mitigated Variant: Presentation

Like the pure type of the bipolar-confrontational conception, the mitigated variant is patterned on cold war premises rather than on notions related to North-South relations or derived from regional or local paradigms. It is therefore predisposed to perceive the world in terms of the *overall* balance of power. American statesmen and diplomats who approximate this category tend to see in the great-power relationship the master key to world order. Hence, they continuously underscore "the connection between the local situation and the great powers' contest;"[33] they insist that "the actions of a major power are inevitably related to and have consequences beyond the issue or region immediately

19

concerned,"[34] and that "events in different parts of the world [are] related to each other."[35] Here the mitigated bipolar-confrontational approach shares with its pure counterpart the propensity to promote local issues to the superpower level, and thus to relate limited conflicts to the global balance of power. As a result of this preoccupation with the dynamics of the bipolar conflict, policymakers of this type tend to impose on regional events global categories of thought. They apply to disputes like the Arab-Israel conflict the yardstick of the Soviet-American contest by projecting on them "the anxiety derived from the real or imaginary links that might exist between the ratio of forces in conflict in the area and the ratio of the superpowers' forces."[36]

Referring to representatives of this approach, Garthoff writes:

> Even the most...geopolitical or realistic American leaders, Nixon and Kissinger, saw the Syrian-Jordanian clash of 1970 and the Indo-Pakistani War of 1971 as Soviet proxy wars. Later Kissinger conceded that the fall of South Vietnam in 1975, and the adverse...situation in Portugal in mid-1975, were not caused by Soviet machinations but by "internal dynamics." But even then he saw these situations as ulti-mately determined by Soviet and American actions, and faulted the United States for not having done more.[37]

However, unlike the pure bipolar-confrontational tendency to view the balance of power as a "zero-sum game," in which "gains" for one side invariably mean "losses" for the other, the mitigated form of this foreign policy orientation (which, in various man-ifestations, is similar to what Dallin and Lapidus define as a "mechanistic" approach and to what Schneider calls a "balance of power" orientation), is predisposed to focus on the *overall* calculus of power. It is therefore prepared on occasion to "trade" what might appear as a loss in one area for gains in another.[38]

Thus, whereas the pure version of the bipolar- confrontational category does not differentiate between the vital and the peripher-al (depicting all interests as vital and all threats as deadly), the mitigated variant establishes hierarchies of interests and threats. It insists on a "strongpoint" defense, concentrating on areas perceived as both vital and defensible (including the Middle East), while tolerating the loss of peripheral areas, providing this does not impair the American ability to defend those areas that are vital.[39] In other words, while bipolar-confrontational decision-makers of the unmitigated type tend to resist *any* attempt to disrupt the global balance of power, the representatives of the modified category tolerate some disengagement.[40]

In the Middle East, however, the parameters within which superpower cooperation and mutual concessions could take place, were severely constrained once that region was regarded as one of "those areas of the world which [the US] cannot permit to fall into hands hostile to us...."[41] Thus Secretary of State Henry Kissinger, who clearly exemplifies this approach, reconstructed the Middle East policy he pursued in the course of the June 1973 San Clemente summit with Brezhnev and acknowledged that "we were prepared to discuss overall principles with Moscow in consultation with our ally Israel and, for that matter, with Egypt, with which preliminary talks had already started. But we were not willing to pay for detente in the coin of our geopolitical position."[42]

Indeed, the Middle East was hardly the ideal locale for developing explicit rules of superpower restraint and crisis prevention, let alone for jointly shaping the parameters of a comprehensive settlement. George defines it as an area of disputed high-interest symmetry, and it is depicted by bipolar-confrontational statesmen (of both types) as an area in which both superpowers have very strong interests, on the relative balance of which they could not agree. It is hardly surprising, then, that by virtue of this pervasive regional perception, the Middle East proved to be the stage for fierce superpower competition during and following the Yom Kippur War. At least prior to the election of Jimmy Carter as president in 1976, superpower cooperation was confined strictly to "dissociative" strategies of crisis management.[43]

Another major tenet of the mitigated variant of bipolarity which sets this category apart from the pure version, is inherent in its quest for containment through negotiation and manipulation rather than through exclusive reliance on strategies of coercion and deterrence. Representatives of this foreign policy orientation seek to proceed from conventional, simplistic formulas and definitions of containment toward more refined and multidimensional structures and definitions. Their vision of the international environment is relatively pluralistic and heterogeneous when juxtaposed with the monolithic and homogeneous pure bipolar-confrontational perception. As Kissinger noted: "It is always tempting to arrange diverse Soviet moves into a grand design. The more esoteric books of Kremlinology often purport to see each and every move as part of a carefully orchestrated score in which events inexorably move to the grand finale. Experience has shown that this has rarely been the case."[44]

Still, the concept of containment has remained central to the mitigated approach, albeit in a less stolid and simplistic form than in its pure counterpart.[45] Thus, in seeking to combat the frightening vision of escalation and superpower confrontation which is inherent in the pursuit of a pure bipolar-confrontational posture, the architects of the mitigated form of bipolarity have predicated their notion of containment on a combination of both threats and incentives, designed to induce the Soviet rival to moderate certain of its foreign policy behavioral patterns.[46] Typically, in Kissinger's words: "We are in favor of detente because we want to limit the risks of major nuclear conflict."[47]

Whereas the Reaganite pure version relied exclusively on threats and penalties as operational tools, the Kissingerian mitigated approach was based on a combination of pressures and inducements that could, if successful, have convinced the Russians that it was in their own best interests to be "contained."[48] Advocates of this approach sought to entangle the Soviets in a complex web of incentives and penalties and thus to integrate them as a stable and reconciled element into the existing world order (in the hope of eventually building on the resulting equilibrium a less competitive "structure of peace"). They based their strategy on Moscow's interest in trade, access to western credit, grain, and technology.

In the words of Stanley Hoffmann:

[Nixon and Kissinger] were far more willing than any of their predecessors...to obtain what could be called containment by negotiation. Indeed, the failure to engage the Soviets in negotiations at a time when the United States was comparatively stronger is one of Kissinger's chief criticisms of early cold-war policies....What Nixon and Kissinger appeared to want was really quite grandiose: a far more diversified use of means, a complex system of incentives and sanctions aimed at inducing Soviet self-containment, and a conception of international order to provide the previously missing "content." The design tried to synthesize adversary containment with the "friendly embrace" — or ensnaring — that Roosevelt had had in mind; but Kissinger and Nixon recognized his illusions, and they were far more determined to use all the levers of power.[49]

Thus, unlike the determinist and utterly pessimistic nature of the pure approach, in which the entire array of international interactions is portrayed as an endless cycle of pressures and counterpressures between two irreconcilable entities, the mitigated variant was patterned on the more optimistic premise that the fundamental clash of ideologies between the two superpowers could be "managed" into coexistence (which itself could later be molded into a more positive and cooperative future): "By acquiring a stake in this network of relationships with the West," observed Kissinger in 1974, the Soviet Union may become more conscious of what it would lose by a return to confrontation. "Indeed, it is our expectation," he concluded, "that it will develop a self-interest in fostering the entire process of relaxation of tensions."[50]

On a global scale this somewhat Pavlovian scheme of behavior modification — the offering of rewards and penalties to the Soviet opponent in the hope of inducing restraint — by definition implied that issues were interrelated; consequently, agreement had to be reached on "a broad range of issues," lest an isolated deal fall victim to the other surrounding conflicts. As Garthoff points out,

One seeks to move a recalcitrant animal by offering mutually reinforcing positive incentives pointed in the desired direction, coupled with negative sanctions if it does not move. More basically, the entire thrust of Kissinger's strategy of detente was one of maneuver in a shifting global balance of power that was becoming increasingly akin to the classical multipolar structure of the eighteenth and nineteenth centuries, albeit now with two predominant powers.[51]

Specifically, a mitigated bipolar-confrontational strategy of the sort that the Nixon administration pursued with much vigor after its inauguration in 1969, sought to envelop the Soviets in a network of economic and political ties with the West that would deepen their material stake in continued collaboration, thus promoting ever-growing Soviet restraint in the fiercely competitive game played in third areas as well as in Berlin.[52] As Kissinger asserted as early as February 18, 1969: "I am convinced that the great issues are fundamentally inter-related....I believe that the Soviet leaders should be brought to understand that they cannot expect to reap the benefits of cooperation in one area while seeking to take advantage of tension or confrontation elsewhere."[53]

More than five years later, this perception of organic linkage remained intact:

Our approach proceeds from the conviction that, in moving forward across a wide spectrum of negotiations, progress in one area adds momentum to progress in other areas. If we succeed, then no agreement stands alone as an isolated accomplishment vulnerable to the next crisis. We did not invent the interrelationship between issues expressed in the so-called linkage concept; it was a reality because of the range of problems and areas in which the interests of the United States and the Soviet Union impinge on one another.[54]

And in the words of Richard Nixon, which translate these refined formulations into tangible policy objectives:

During the transition period (following the presidential election of 1968) Kissinger and I developed a new policy for dealing with the Soviets. Since US-Soviet interests in the world's two competing nuclear superpowers were so widespread and overlapping, it was unrealistic to separate or compartmentalize areas of concern. Therefore we decided to link progress in such areas of concern as strategic arms limitation and increased trade with progress in areas that were important to us — Vietnam, the Mideast, and Berlin. This concept became known as linkage.[55]

By virtue of its insistence on the need to redefine containment in a manner which incorporates a cluster of positive inducements into an essentially competitive framework, the mitigated variant of bipolarity, unlike the pure version, is fully compatible with the notion of superpower negotiations on a wide range of controversial issues. Combined with the notion of linkage — which implies that a setback for one of the superpowers in a given locale or on a specific issue can be tolerated provided compensation in kind is found — this foreign policy category creates new opportunities for superpower collaboration on the shaping and parameters of local settlements, or on specific trade-offs in their bilateral relations with regional clients, allies and proxies. However, since even in this modified version of the bipolar approach, the international system is still perceived as essentially dichotomous, with the Soviet Union depicted as an ambitious antagonist, trade-offs are bound to remain confined strictly to areas of secondary importance or to issues about which a mutual interest in regulating competition is strong enough to prevail over suspicion.

Predicated upon a perception of a highly competitive environment, in which the Soviet adversary could only gradually be "cajoled into accepting the 'legitimacy' of the international order,"[56] the mitigated bipolar perspective ruled out the possibility that the US and the Soviet Union would agree "to general purpose rules of engagement that are intended to apply across the board to all areas and situations in which the two superpowers may find themselves in competition." According to this perception, "detente is thus strongest in areas of negotiated mutual benefits — trade and arms control. It is weakest where the interests are too sensitive, asymmetrical, and diffuse to be negotiated."[57]

Thus, for all their aspirations "to reduce the level of conflict behavior and hostility, and to maximize cooperation where cooperation is feasible," the architects of the mitigated bipolar orientation insisted on a highly limited definition of their overall design. This held that detente between the superpowers could not lead to entente or alliance, nor could it ever develop into a condominium. The rivalry between the two superpowers could well be mitigated, but it could not completely disappear.[58]

Kissinger's Exclusionist Diplomacy and the Mitigated Variant: Application

Kissinger's Middle East diplomacy as it unfolded during and immediately following the Yom Kippur War, was closely patterned on the premises of mitigated bipolarity. Clearly, the parameters within which superpower cooperation for defusing the Arab-Israel conflict could be achieved in this area of disputed high-interest symmetry were severely constrained. It is true that American diplomacy did attempt on occasion (particularly on the declarative level) to reconcile the collaborative elements of the mitigated variant of bipolarity it pursued with the reality of fierce big-power competition in the Middle East. However, the way in which the issues were resolved did not involve any unilateral sacrifices or concessions to the Soviet Union; nor did it precipitate a regional policy of condominium, whereby victory would be shared with the Soviet rival through an arrangement in which both sides would gain part of the interests in contention. Instead, fully committed to the mitigated bipolar-confrontational notions of linkage and interdependence, the architects of American Middle East policy were prepared to offer Moscow a wide range of economic incentives *outside* the area in return for its restraint, or — better still — acquiescence in the face of unilateral American gains. As Kissinger observed in his memoirs in alluding to the pre-war period: "To be sure, Moscow in mid-1972 had good reasons of its own for not rocking the Middle East boat. It desperately needed to purchase American grain. It may have concluded that to add a Middle East crisis to the war in Vietnam might shred the gossamer fabric of East-West relations....The Soviets were willing to pay *some* price for detente."[59] Similarly, during the period immediately following the war, in an attempt to secure Soviet acquiescence in the face of his unilateral Middle East initiatives, Kissinger used American grain sales as a lever on Soviet Middle East policy and as an incentive "to conduct moderate foreign policies."[60] In general, in reconstructing the bounds within which the mitigated variant of bipolarity was implemented in the Middle East following the outbreak of the Yom Kippur War, it is clear that *actual* superpower cooperation never exceeded the level of crisis-management.

This propensity of the Nixon presidency to minimize the scope of American-Soviet collaboration in the wake of the 1973 conflagration and to proceed unilaterally in the quest for peace, marked a major deviation from the administration's early overtures toward the Soviet Union.

Culminating in the Two-Power talks of 1969 on the parameters of a comprehensive settlement, these intensive, yet ultimately abortive, negotiations, reflected the priorities and preconceptions of the State Department, which for various reasons was encouraged by President Nixon to play a dominant role in forging a regional peace strategy which clearly contradicted some of his mitigated bipolar-confrontational premises.[61] A mitigated bipolar-confrontational orientation (of the sort which was pursued in the Middle East from 1973-1975) insists that any superpower trade-offs not involve the sacrifice of vital security areas (unless the perceived alternative is the highly menacing prospect of a superpower confrontation), but be confined strictly to the periphery of the international system. In stark contrast, the strategy launched in 1969 by Secretary of State William Rogers was based on an entirely different form of linkage, namely, on a perception of the Middle East as "a lever to pry loose some Soviet cooperation on Vietnam."[62] Indeed, Rogers was convinced that negotiations with the Soviet Union and countries aligned with the Kremlin could well lead to accommodation and the amelioration of international

26

tension, and so embarked upon a major initiative — the Rogers Plan — in which the United States sought an agreement on general principles with the Soviets for comprehensively settling the dispute.

Soon after, however, with the outbreak in 1969 of the Israeli-Egyptian War of Attrition, and the subsequent intensification of the Soviet military role in Egypt, this notion of a Middle East-Vietnam trade-off with the Soviet Union was abandoned. Faced with these threatening developments, as well as with continued Israeli opposition to Rogers' initiatives, President Nixon and his national security adviser ultimately ruled out the possibility of any unilateral American concessions in the Middle East, regardless of the nature of the compensation offered elsewhere. Instead, they insisted on a reverse form of linkage — between Moscow's acquiescence in the area and American compensation elsewhere.

Indeed, during the years 1970-1972, not only did the Nixon administration resort to strictly exclusionist mediation strategies (such as the abortive drive of May 1971 to conclude an interim agreement between Egypt and Israel, or the ceasefire initiative which terminated the War of Attrition) in the hope of stabilizing the Egyptian-Israeli front, but it became increasingly motivated by an acutely threatening vision of Soviet domination in the Middle East. Thus as early as July 2, 1970, Kissinger stated: "We are trying to expel the Soviet military presence, not so much the advisers, but the combat personnel, the combat pilots, before they become so firmly established."[63]

In embarking on his post-Yom Kippur War strategy, Kissinger recognized the need to set aside the tools of conventional diplomacy. While operating formally within the parameters of US strategic goals, Kissinger sought to proceed from the simplistic formulas and definitions of "containment" and "peace" to more subtle and multidimensional structures.

Earlier, such pure bipolar-confrontational statesmen as Secretary of State John Foster Dulles had based their Middle East policy on one single and sharply delineated premise to which they clung tenaciously and irreversibly, even when it meant the de facto abandonment of other desired goals. Kissinger, on the other hand, was always careful to define US strategic objectives in a manner which enabled him to pursue several objectives simultaneously. Indeed, in the pure bipolar-confrontational type, the need to contain Soviet encroachment invariably outweighs a second traditional US objective: the search for regional accommodation. By comparison, Kissinger's muted version of bipolarity viewed both of these cardinal goals not as incompatible alternative policy options, but rather as interrelated objectives which could be reconciled and integrated into a coherent and multifaceted American regional policy.

What was particularly novel in this enterprise was Kissinger's reliance on the step-by-step method as his major tactical tool for promoting American strategic goals. Not only did this minimize the danger of a direct superpower conflagration in the Middle East, but it enabled the US to proceed uninterruptedly toward the accomplishment of its entire design in the Arab-Israeli sphere.

It may, of course, be argued that a mitigated bipolar confrontational strategy is not the only approach amenable to step-by-step diplomacy as Kissinger practiced it — i.e., that step-by-step might be implemented in concert with the Soviets within the framework of an accommodative posture. But, as we shall see, Kissinger himself clearly felt that the step-by-step tactic was an exclusionist device, even when he made public declarations which seemed to imply a more accommodative view.

Kissinger's reliance on gradual change as his chief unilateral instrument was derived from his perceptions of both the Middle Eastern subsystem and the global international system. On the regional level, he was clearly motivated by the conviction that in order to defuse the intense Arab-Israel conflict, it was necessary to proceed gradually. Given the complexity of the question at hand, he believed that the introduction of "theoretical and comprehensive formulas" for settling the entire problem "with a single stroke" could only expose and sharpen irreconcilable differences and thus aggravate a situation already fraught with tension. As he pointed out in September 1975:

> ...for 30 years it proved nearly impossible even to begin the process of negotiation. Every attempt to discuss a comprehensive solution failed — from the partition plan, to the Lausanne Conference [1949], to the Rogers Plan and the Four-Power talks of 1969 and 1970, to the UN Security Council deliberations. *To discuss simultaneously issues of such complexity, between countries whose deep mutual mistrust rejected even the concept of compromise was futile until a minimum of confidence had been established.*[64]

Indeed, step-by-step diplomacy offered no grand design for

resolving the Arab-Israeli predicament. It deliberately avoided even suggesting what the eventual shape of an overall settlement might be. Instead,

step-by-step sought to maintain a minimum stability, stability to be achieved through a series of limited agreements that left ambiguous the shape of the ultimate outcome....Limited agreements might serve progressively to narrow the initially profound differences separating adversaries, while slowly establishing an increasing measure of trust and confidence.[65]

Believing that if conducted properly, negotiations could take on a momentum of their own which would eventually facilitate an overall agreement, Kissinger was predisposed to side-step emotion-laden issues in favor of a series of quid pro quos in less controversial areas of mutual interest. It was essential, then, to "reduce problems to manageable proportions" which could be negotiated separately. Such segmentation, he hoped, "would permit each party to adjust itself domestically and internationally to a process of a gradual approach toward peace."[66] Stein writes:

Kissinger built the bargaining agenda carefully. Beginning generally with the issues most amenable to solution, he postponed indefinitely those he considered most resistant to compromise, expecting that progress in negotiation would itself generate momentum and change the bargaining environment to permit further progress. What he kept off the agenda was far more important than what he put on the table.[67]

In the course of his negotiations with the Chinese, Kissinger concentrated first on areas of mutual interest, and delayed consideration of difficult issues like the status of Taiwan and the future of diplomatic relations. Similarly, he was determined to avoid an early entanglement with the knottiest issues of the Middle East conflict. As Spiegel observes,

consistent with his prewar policy, Kissinger hoped US influence could be increased by interim agreements that skirted the fundamental questions. Therefore, he tried as far as possible to avoid the thorny issues: the Palestinian question, the final Israeli borders, and the nature of the peace after the negotiations....The war and Sadat's interest in improving relations with the United States gave Kissinger the opportunity to achieve this strategy.[68]

Because each of the individual, incremental steps taken in the

Middle East deviated only marginally from the existing status quo, they could be presented and "sold" to critics on both sides as insignificant moves which did not entail any real changes in that country's foreign policy. The step-by-step approach was therefore an expedient device for neutralizing both domestic and external opposition and obstructionism. Likewise, on the global level, by virtue of its unobtrusiveness and gradualism, Kissinger's strategy reduced the possibility of a potentially dangerous Soviet retaliation.

This perception of the negotiating process as "a psychological drive" precluded any shortcut of the sort that the Rogers Plan sought to implement. Only if, following a prolonged process of reassuring interactions, both parties were emotionally prepared to abandon "passionate ideologies" and irreconcilable dogmas for the sake of adopting a more pragmatic approach, would a formal construction of the terms of peace have any hope of implementation.[69] Thus a prolonged diplomatic process which benefited both parties — with the US providing material incentives and compensation for concessions made — was perceived as the optimal means for bringing about substantial changes in attitudes and thereby, ultimately, in the nature of the conflict. Kissinger's report after successfully negotiating a disengagement agreement between Syria and Israel is illustrative:

> During recent months the first crucial steps have been taken to break this impasse. Thanks to the farsighted views of key leaders in the region, and with the active role of the United States, we have seen important steps toward peace and the *partial erosion of decades of hostility and mistrust among the parties.*[70]

Notwithstanding this propensity to proceed in a piecemeal fashion and to obfuscate the magnitude of progress made, it was expected that when completed, this entire aggregate process would represent a far-reaching departure from initial postures and attitudes. In other words, the eventual culmination of the process would in fact mean its disappearance as an operational tool for advancing a settlement. With the parties capable of assimilating new perceptions and of taking "a risk for peace,"[71] there would no longer be any need to minimize the entire scope and ramifications of changes which had taken place gradually.

In applying this intricate conceptual design to the concrete circumstances of the volatile Middle East during the period following the 1973 war, Kissinger's diplomacy was articulated on two levels. In private and confidential exchanges and briefings, he was quite assertive in presenting the step-by-step approach as an exclusionist tactical device, designed to reduce Soviet regional influence.[72] On these occasions, he continuously argued that the US was determined to expel the Soviets from the Middle East, and deny them a victory in the region.[73] As he acknowledged retrospectively:

> I had always believed it essential to reduce the scope of Soviet adventurist policies in the Middle East....I thought the prerequisite of effective Middle East diplomacy was to reduce the Soviet influence so that progress could not be ascribed to its pressures and moderate governments gained some maneuvering room....I was...profoundly distrustful of Soviet motives, determined to prevent Soviet expansion, scornful of those critics who abjectly accepted Soviet advances or relied on history to undo them. To some extent my interest in detente was tactical, as a device to maximize Soviet dilemmas and reduce Soviet influence in the Middle East.[74]

Similarly, in a meeting with King Faisal in Riyadh in November 1973, Kissinger stated: "I wish to explain our actions in the war of last month....We were motivated by a desire to prevent an increase of Communist influence, and when the Soviets began to send in arms, we had to react."[75] Indeed, during the period immediately following the war, Kissinger embarked on an ambitious "exclusionist diplomacy," designed to advance his mitigated bipolar-confrontational world view in the Middle East.[76]

Notwithstanding the unilateralist nature of Kissinger's entire design, his *public* statements regarding the Soviet role in a Middle East settlement were much more conciliatory than those of several of his bipolar-confrontational predecessors. Hoping to utilize the accommodative component of his mitigated approach as "a tranquilizer for Moscow as we sought to draw the Middle East into closer relations with us at the Soviet's expense," and convinced that an open, undisguised maximalist posture toward Soviet interests was bound to trigger the Soviets into recalcitrant behavior and "a political assault on us in the Middle East,"[77] he consistently endeavored to minimize the nature of his overall design. As Hoffmann points out, there was a clear contradiction between the appearance of a US-Soviet condominium, which the two sets of principles adopted in the summits of 1972 and 1973 could not fail to suggest, and the far more profound reality of implacable containment, of intractable hostility to the expansion of Soviet influence. However much Nixon and Kissinger *sounded*, in each case, as though they wanted cooperation and accommodation, they *acted* on the premises of unending, if manageable, rivalry.[78]

For example, shortly after agreeing, during the final phases of the 1973 war, to establish a multilateral forum (the Geneva Conference) under US-Soviet cochairmanship for negotiating a Middle East settlement, Kissinger sidestepped the Geneva forum and opted for a series of unilateral negotiating steps. He hoped that by segmenting his diplomacy (while still giving the Soviets a sense of participation) "the Soviet capacity for obstruction would be at a minimum."[79] In this way he ultimately succeeded in transforming the Geneva framework into a symbolic umbrella, under which he effectively played the role of sole mediator in bilateral negotiations between Israel and Egypt that culminated in the January 1974 disengagement agreement.

However, alongside this unwavering determination to reduce the Geneva gathering to a merely "symbolic act,"[80] Kissinger offered, in his public statements of late December (the period in which the conference was held), an entirely different image of the significance of the conference both to the peacemaking effort and regarding the Soviet role in the diplomatic process. Thus, in addressing the conference on December 2, 1973 he was euphoric:

> We are convened here at the moment of historic opportunity for the cause of peace in the Middle East, and for the cause of peace in the world. For the first time in a generation, the peoples of the Middle East are sitting together to turn their talents to the challenge of a lasting peace....Progress toward peace should include *all* parties concerned.[81]

Similarly, in his press conference of December 24, 1973, he asserted:

> We believe that in setting up the [Geneva] conference, and in helping to define possible agendas, participation, framework, the Soviet Union has played a constructive role. A settlement in the Middle East cannot be carried out without the Soviet Union, the principal supplier of arms to several of the participants — and given its close association with and friendship with several of the countries.[82]

32

Again, in the spring of 1974 Kissinger set out rhetorically to counterbalance what appeared to be a vigorous exclusionist initiative to regain American influence in the region and establish new channels of communication with Syria and Iraq. In his public statements he consistently offered a minimalist interpretation of American diplomacy. For example, in his press conference of June 6, 1974, following the conclusion of the Syrian-Israeli disengagement agreement, the secretary emphatically downplayed the significance of his mediation, maintaining that:

> Obviously the Middle East is an area of great concern to the Soviet Union....We do not believe that the influence of a country in the Middle East is directly related to who conducts a particular negotiation....As we go into the next phase of negotiations in the Middle East, which will *certainly* involve the Geneva forum in some manner, the Soviet Union participates in that as the co-chairman of the Geneva Conference. And in any event, whatever the Soviet role in a particular negotiation, there is no American intention of expelling the Soviet Union from the Middle East.[83]

Such public reassurances and conciliatory rhetoric were patterned on the accommodative premises of Kissinger's mitigated bipolar outlook. In contrast, his concurrent confidential communications — which were all exclusionist in nature — derived from the coercive components of his inherently dual strategy of "firmness and conciliation."[84] It was the cover of conciliation (incorporating promises for incentives and compensations to the Soviets outside the Middle East) which enabled American diplomacy "to make progress" in the area while at the same time avoiding "an open confrontation with the Soviets...at a point of maximum weakness to our executive authority."[85] But there can be little doubt as to which dimension of this mitigated version of the bipolar-confrontational approach was assigned priority within the confines of the Arab-Israeli predicament. As Kissinger pointed out in a memorandum to President Nixon on April 12, 1974 — during the period immediately preceding conclusion of the Syrian-Israeli disengagement agreement:

> Any direct Soviet participation in Middle East negotiations would inevitably greatly reduce the chances of success in bringing peace to the area. For one thing, Sadat and Asad as well as Israel want to keep them out. For another, they want to lump all the issues together in one big negotiation at

Geneva, and we believe the whole process will stall unless we can continue to segment the negotiation into politically manageable units. Thus *we must continue to exclude the Soviets, while at the same time publicly minimizing their exclusion and privately reassuring them of our intention to keep them informed at every step of the negotiations.* We are prepared to discuss the Syrian-Israeli disengagement in a general way or to discuss in theory the future role of the Geneva Conference, but we do not want to get into such detail as to enable the Soviets to build resistance to specific proposals.[86]

Fully committed to their premises, members of Washington's high policy elite, while seeking to convince the Soviet leadership that "nothing was further from [its] mind...than to exclude Moscow...[and that] our whole strategy was designed to enable the Soviets to play a significant role,"[87] embarked on the next phase of negotiations, which did not in fact involve either the Geneva forum or the Soviet Union in any significant way.

Indeed, notwithstanding the joint superpower communique of February 17, 1975, in which Kissinger and Gromyko reiterated their belief that "the Geneva Conference should play an important part in the establishment of a joint and lasting peace in the Middle East, and should resume its work at an early date,"[88] the secretary of state continued undeterred in his search for an interim agreement in the Sinai Peninsula between Egypt and Israel. There followed a protracted and complicated round of exclusionist diplomacy which culminated in the conclusion, on September 1, 1975, of the Sinai II accord between Egypt and Israel. Here Kissinger was similarly modest and accommodative in his public assessment:

In the Middle East I do not believe that the essential interests of the United States and the Soviet Union are in any sense incompatible. I do not believe that the recent agreement beween Egypt and Israel is in any sense detrimental to the interests of the Soviet Union or a unilateral advantage for the United States. The significance of the agreement is that it defuses the tensions in the area and if it is implemented properly will open, or can open, a door to general peace in the area. And if we consider that every war in the Middle East has involved the danger of confrontation of the two nuclear superpowers, it is in the mutual interests of both the Soviet

Union and the United States to reduce the tensions of war. The United States recognizes that in a final settlement in the Middle East, a Soviet role will be important; and therefore we are debating now certain procedural questions about the Soviet role in the recent negotiations — rather than a unilateral advantage gained by the United States at the expense of the Soviet Union.[89]

This statement, like the one sixteen months before, was couched in terms which did not commit the US to any specific move vis-à-vis the Soviet Union. Following the patterns which he established during the Israeli-Egyptian disengagement negotiations, Kissinger continued to procrastinate on any discussion of the major controversial issues of the conflict. Fearing that a multilateral, comprehensive peacemaking approach was bound to aggravate a situation already fraught with tension and stress by enabling the Soviet Union "to inject itself as the lawyer of the Arab side," he continued to rely on unilateral step-by-step diplomacy. Thus Washington's policymakers ultimately succeeded in diverting negotiation of concrete issues into bilateral channels in which Kissinger continuously played the role of go-between and mediator between the parties, while at the same time hoping "to give the Soviets enough of a sense of participation to prevent them from disrupting the peace effort."[90]

Only on those infrequent occasions when the US perceived a convergence of interests on certain delimited issues — e.g., the need to terminate the Yom Kippur War before the regional balance of power was completely altered — was this unilateral American approach modified. Such phases of cooperation were always aimed at defusing isolated segments of the conflict (rather than at mitigating the entire Arab-Israeli predicament), and as such never exceeded the level of crisis management.

The Geneva option was useful to Kissinger in more ways than one. Apart from seeking to reassure the Soviets of a future role in the peacemaking process, Kissinger raised the specter of reconvening the Geneva Peace Conference (of which the Soviet Union was cochairman) in order to soften Israel's opposition to several schemes he formulated in the course of his shuttles. His repeated invocation of this unpleasant alternative (in Israel's eyes) to the exclusionist, step-by-step approach during his abortive mission in February-March 1975, is clearly documented by Sheehan. Discussing in Jerusalem the ramifications which, in his view, were likely to result from a failure to conclude an interim agreement in Sinai, Kissinger predicted:

> I don't see how there can be another American initiative in the near future. We may have to go to Geneva for a multilateral effort with the Soviets — something which for five years we've felt did not offer the best hope for success ....We're losing control. We'll now see the Arabs working on a united front. There will be more emphasis on the Palestinians, and there will be linkage between moves in the Sinai and on the Golan. The Soviets will step back onto the stage. The United States is losing control over events, and we'd all better adjust ourselves to that reality.[91]

On the whole, Kissinger's Middle East policy was not less ambitious or maximalist than the posture advanced by the US during most of the Cold War era. And although he attempted to incorporate his policy into the framework of mitigated bipolarity, in practice he pursued an incremental undermining of Soviet strongholds in the area:

> After an initial effort during the first year or two of the Nixon administration to find a basis for diplomatic cooperation with the Soviet Union in settling the Arab-Israeli conflict, first Washington and then Moscow pursued divergent objectives and strategies that in effect ruled out cooperation between them in the interests of crisis prevention. Even while ostensibly seeking a cooperative solution, each superpower covertly pursued a self-seeking unilateral policy of its own toward the Middle East conflict — the United States seeking to bring about a reversal of alliances that would exclude Soviet influence in Egypt, the Soviet Union arming Egypt and Syria and condoning their resort to war....In the aftermath of the October War...Kissinger moved quickly to establish himself at the hub of diplomatic efforts to bring about a disengagement of forces. With Egypt now looking to the United States...Kissinger was able to exclude Moscow from the real negotiations, forcing it to be content with symbolic equality as co-chair with the United States of the Geneva Conference.[92]

On one occasion only was this discrepancy between rhetoric and action, between the proclaimed and the pursued, momentarily resolved. During the last week of the Yom Kippur War Kissinger, faced with mounting indications of accelerated Soviet preparations for the transport of Soviet troops to the area, ultimately resorted to a global nuclear alert. Earlier, on October 24, 1973, following Brezhnev's menacing proposal to "urgently dispatch to Egypt Soviet and American military contingents to ensure the implementation of the Security Council cease-fire resolutions" — coupled with a veiled threat of possible unilateral Soviet action if the US refused to collaborate with the Soviet Union — Kissinger warned:

There are limits beyond which we cannot go...we will oppose the attempt by any country to achieve a position of predominance, either globally or regionally....We would resist any attempt to exploit a policy of detente to weaken our alliances ....It is easy to start confrontations, but in this age we have to know where we will be at the end and not only what pose to strike at the beginning....It is inconceivable that we should transplant the great-power rivalry into the Middle East or, alternatively, that we should impose a military condominium by the United States and the Soviet Union. *The United States is even more opposed to the unilateral introduction by any great power, especially by any nuclear power of military forces into the Middle East in whatever guise those forces should be introduced.*[93]

As soon as the tension receded and the ceasefire was effectively enforced, Kissinger moved to mitigate tensions and reaffirm the need for superpower cooperation. On December 27, 1973, he intimated:

It has been demonstrated that the conflict in the Middle East can bring the superpowers into positions of potential confrontation. And it is therefore at least possible that the Soviet Union now has an interest in contributing to the stabilization of the situation in any area which neither superpower can really control by itself....That is to say, if the Soviet Union makes a responsible contribution to peace in the Middle East, we will be prepared to cooperate....We are in direct contact with all of the parties in the Middle East. But we are prepared to deal with the Soviet Union on an equitable basis as long as its motives — or as long as its actions — are consistent with a responsible course.[94]

Reaffirming further that his mitigated bipolar-confrontational orientation incorporated "an element both of cooperation and of competition," and as such could easily accommodate various forms of non-military unilateral superpower action, the secretary sought a course which would minimize the risks of a direct clash with Moscow, but which would at the same time improve the American regional position at the expense of the Soviet Union. The exclusionist strategy actually pursued by Kissinger in a piecemeal fashion during most of his tenure as secretary of state appeared to be, at least in the short run, an effective means to this end. US diplomacy succeeded not only in greatly improving relations with Egypt, but also in opening new channels of communication with Syria and Iraq. As Kissinger himself conceded in June 1975:

> In the Middle East I would not be surprised if in Moscow they...said that we have been using detente to improve our position. At any rate it is not evident to me — in contrast to our own position — that the Soviet Union has improved its position in the Middle East in the last two years. The opposite seems to me to be the case.[95]

In conclusion, the intrinsic nature of the mitigated variant of the bipolar-confrontational orientation as implemented in the region by Nixon and Kissinger in the aftermath of the Yom Kippur War, precluded the possibility of a superpower condominium. Although not as dichotomous in its world view and perceptions of the Soviet adversary as the pure bipolar-confrontational variant, this approach relied largely, in the Middle East, on the principles of deterrence and coercive diplomacy, and used accommodative gestures as a tactical, ritualistic incentive to placate the Soviets. It was premised on the conviction that Soviet regional aims were hegemonic,[96] and that an unbridgeable gap separated the super-powers' respective visions of the shaping of peace — with Moscow insisting on a multilateral negotiating forum that would simul-taneously tackle all substantive issues and reaffirm its status as a global power, a regional power, and as the primary military and political patron of key Arab states, while Washington opted for a phased, exclusionist peacemaking strategy.[97]

Indeed, taking full advantage of the Soviets' overriding interest in additional benefits from the detente process (inherent in the accommodative components of the mitigated bipolar-confrontational approach) which they were reluctant to damage,[98] Kissinger could proceed with impunity in his exclusionist Middle East diplomacy, fully convinced that the Soviet reaction would fall considerably short of a radical obstructionist posture.[99] In this respect, American post-1973 diplomacy confronted the Soviet

Union with an insoluble dilemma. By linking Soviet acquiescence to their Middle East initiative to the entire structure of detente, American policymakers could offer the Kremlin economic and political incentives "to conduct moderate foreign policies."[100] Furthermore, the very ambivalence of the unilateral but incremental approach which Kissinger pursued, with each step representing but a marginal departure from the preexisting status quo, gave the Soviets few grounds for a superpower confrontation over the Middle East.[101]

Nonetheless, Moscow became increasingly irritated by the successes of Kissinger's exclusionist diplomacy. Thus on April 12, 1974, as Kissinger embarked on his "Syrian shuttle," Soviet Foreign Minister Gromyko resorted to harsh rhetoric in assailing President Nixon for pursuing a "separatist" posture in the area, insisting — as Secretary Brezhnev had done in an earlier conversation with Kissinger on March 25, 1974 — on "full Soviet participation" in the peace process under joint superpower auspices.

Similarly, while over-anxious to avoid a major superpower crisis over the Middle East, the Soviets reacted angrily to the conclusion, on September 1, 1975, of the Sinai interim agreement between Egypt and Israel. Not only did the Soviet press denounce the agreement as a threat to Arab unity, but the Soviet Union boycotted the signing ceremony in Geneva, thereby signaling its displeasure and frustration in the face of the relegation of the Geneva format to a formal, ceremonial framework.[102]

The reality of severely constrained superpower collaboration in the Arab-Israeli sphere also reflected the preference of some of the local protagonists. Indeed, on those infrequent occasions (such as the Two-Power talks), where the architects of American diplomacy attempted momentarily to widen the parameters of superpower collaboration (and thus to deviate from the premises and logic of the mitigated bipolar-confrontational orientation), they were ultimately compelled — as a result of both domestic and external pressures — to forego their intention.[103] Similarly, Secretary Rogers' desire to proceed apace toward comprehensive peace and to solicit Soviet cooperation in order to jointly formulate at least some of the parameters of a settlement, was confronted with staunch Israeli opposition, which culminated in its formal rejection of the Rogers Plan (Egypt also rejected the plan).

In other words, although derived from a global complex of beliefs and attitudes, Kissinger's unilateralist diplomacy did not unfold in a regional vacuum. It benefited from the position of most of the major regional parties, which either fully supported the American peace strategy, or tacitly endorsed some of Kissinger's moves. Moreover, unlike the sharply asymmetrical military situation (and continued polarization between the two superpowers) which emerged along the Arab-Israeli front in the wake of the Six-Day War of June 1967, and which reduced the incentives for both sides to enter into a process of political bargaining, the dangerously unstable military stalemate (combined with a depolarization of the regional conflict) precipitated by the Yom Kippur War of October 1973, was paradoxically conducive to progress in negotiations.

Furthermore, in embarking on his intensive mediation effort, the secretary took advantage of the growing Arab recognition that the "United States could get from Israel what no one else could get."[104] In this respect, the 1973 war constituted the "trigger event" for the establishment of a new pattern in American relations with Egypt and Syria: "The secretary of state wanted a new relationship with the Egyptians and the Syrians as an entree for US influence and interests in the area. He could offer economic aid and the prestige of American attention, but his major bargaining point was the prospect of Israeli concessions."[105] As for Israel, it considered the prospects of an exclusive American mediating effort as considerably less threatening than any multilateral drive. With "Egypt and ultimately Syria [insisting] on our [American] participation," the architects of American Middle East diplomacy managed to secure — at least until September 1975 — a sufficient degree of regional support for the implementation of their exclusionist design.[106]

In embarking on his mediation drive, Kissinger was keenly aware of the structure of the situation, namely, of the compatibility between some of the American regional objectives and the goals of at least some of the local belligerents. Moreover, with Sadat still unprepared, in the aftermath of the war which he had initiated, to proceed toward "positive peace" with Israel, and with Israel adamantly opposed, during Kissinger's entire tenure as secretary of state, to the idea of a complete withdrawal from the Sinai Peninsula, the incremental, at times "creatively ambiguous" implementation of Kissinger's unilateralist approach proved to be the only feasible diplomatic method during the period following the war.[107]

Thus provided with the necessary margin of maneuverability,

the Nixon and Ford foreign policy elites could effectively carry out their mitigated bipolar-confrontational strategy of inducing and enticing the parties to engage in a prolonged process of mutually beneficial interactions, which was expected to ultimately culminate in a comprehensive, permanent peace. Contrary to President Carter's inability to consolidate an external infrastructure of support for his collaborative comprehensive approach — to which the analysis now turns — Kissinger's exclusionist strategy of incremental change succeeded in establishing an adequate base of regional support and legitimacy to pave the way toward the implementation of some of its objectives. From the Israeli viewpoint, for example, this policy was the least objectionable because it obfuscated a cluster of highly controversial questions, which were inextricably related to any discussion of a comprehensive settlement. Similarly, the pattern established by Kissinger relieved the Arabs of the need to negotiate directly with the Israelis or to compensate Israel substantially for the return of territory in the Sinai Peninsula. Thus, in the case of the Sinai Interim Agreement, it was the American mediator — rather than the Egyptian adversary — who offered to Israel a wide assortment of political, economic and military incentives in order to coax it into abandoning most of its demands vis-à-vis Egypt. Indeed, the Israeli withdrawal from the Mitla and Gidi passes and from the oil fields of Abu Rudeis was not reciprocated by any explicit formal Egyptian commitment to terminate the state of belligerency. Israel was not satisfied with Sadat's readiness to offer several "functional equivalents" to formal "non-belligerence." It was the American compensation to Israel, inherent in the logic of Kissinger's unilateralist diplomacy, which provided the impetus for modifying Prime Minister Rabin's position.[108]

Chapter 3. The Multipolar-Accommodative Conception

Presentation

The multipolar-accommodative category approximates, in its various manifestations, what Holsti labels as "Post-Cold War Internationalism," what Yergin terms "The Yalta axioms," what Zimmerman refers to as "an organismic or cybernetic conception," what Dallin and Lapidus define as an "interactionist approach," and what Schneider calls "liberal internationalism."[1] The multipolar-accommodationists perceive an international system which is complex and diverse. In the multipolar vision, East-West relations comprise but one element in a multidimensional environment. Since many of the rivalries and disputes which continuously erupt in this heterogeneous setting are perceived by advocates of this approach as context-dependent and largely autonomous, they are decoupled from the parameters of East-West relations, and their scope is confined initially to the disputing parties, even if the outcome may have an impact on the global interests of the great powers.[2] Whereas bipolar-confrontational leaders are predisposed to see any conflict situation as inherently menacing (and to advocate, therefore, an irreconcilable posture incorporating coercive or deterring elements), multipolar-accommodative statesmen tend, in approaching the international arena, to distinguish between different types of crises and threats to national security. Convinced that not all conflicts involve "a life and death struggle beween the blocs,"[3] they are therefore predisposed to view as menacing only those crises which have a direct bearing upon a narrowly defined cluster of vital interests.

Thus committed to a narrow concept of "self-defense," the advocates of this orientation assert that the United States' role in world affairs "should be primarily an expression of its objective position [size, wealth] and no more, and that there are severe limits to what even the most powerful nation can and should expect to accomplish."[4] Hence, "especially discriminating selectivity should be exercised in limiting security commitments to the indispensable minimum."[5] Regional conflicts should therefore be dealt with on their own terms and their own merits "by taking into account local and regional realities and no longer, as in Kissinger's days, by applying...the yardstick of the Soviet-American contest."[6]

This approach implies a rejection of the tight bipolar confrontational view of the world. Indeed, a central tenet of the multipolar-accommodative orientation is the predisposition to set aside an entire complex of geopolitical considerations related to superpower rivalries and to the overall political and military balance of power — hence to downgrade the competitive aspect of relations between the superpowers — in favor of a more benign, less combative global perspective centered on economic problems. This multipolar perspective evolves around "the ties of economic interdependence between the South, whose supply of natural resources [is] essential to Northern industries, and the North, whose economic recovery and support for international trade and investment [are] essential for the development of the South in an interdependent world economy."[7] Thus convinced that the dangers arising from strategic and military issues between East and West constitute but one element in a "multidimensional game," representatives of the multipolar-accommodative category in fact argue that the international system is of such complexity and diversity as to render totally obsolete the bipolar vision of a world divided by superpower cleavages and fraught with tension. In the words of Vice President Walter Mondale: "Our policy must recognize that the cleavage between North and South is as important as between East and West."[8]

Thus did the axis of North-South relations become a major concern for members of the Carter entourage, replacing the bipolar-confrontational preoccupation with East-West relations held by previous administrations. A new kind of globalism emerged, one predisposed to underscore the non-military issues comprising North-South relations. The Carter administration — which indeed provides a clear illustration of the multipolar-accommodative foreign policy orientation — believed that "the unifying threat of conflict with the Soviet Union has become less intensive," and was therefore prepared not only to decouple superpower rivalry from a welter of local and regional issues, but to embark on a course which was free from the "inordinate fear" of communism. "A flaw in our foreign policy during [the Nixon era]," observed Secretary of State Cyrus Vance,

> was that it was too narrowly rooted in the concept of an overarching US-Soviet 'geopolitical' struggle....Our national

interests encompassed more than US-Soviet relations ....Many developments did not fit as neatly into an East-West context...it also had become essential for the United States to grapple with the North-South issues — the interwoven problems of the industrialized and nonindustrialized nations.[9]

Whereas the Nixon and Ford administrations pursued a posture which sought to integrate a number of accommodative ingredients and dimensions into a mitigated version of bipolarity; and whereas the Reagan presidency was, at least initially, committed to the logic of a pure bipolar-confrontational orientation — the Carter presidency perceived the international system as composed of a multitude of diverse poles and foci of disturbance. It therefore attempted to pursue an essentially accommodative posture toward Moscow by decoupling a wide range of international crises from the prism of East-West competition.

President Carter decided at the outset to lower the profile and reduce the substance of American-Soviet relations. The administration assigned priority to relations with the economically undeveloped Third World (as well as with other western industrial powers, including Japan). Leading members of the Carter entourage consistently advocated that American diplomacy respond to

the manifold sources of conflict [in the developing world] which arise out of tribal, religious, and ethnic border disputes...in their local terms, i.e., with an awareness of their local significance...and not purely in the game theory projection of the East-West encounter. One of the vulnerabilities we have...in our recent experience is that we have not done so in these terms. We have been inclined to see these manifold problems primarily in their East-West context without sufficient appreciation of the local factors.[10]

The corollary of this considerably more benevolent vision of the Soviet Union and this propensity to deemphasize the competitive dimension of superpower relations, was a diminished preoccupation with the dangers of communism worldwide and an increased willingness not only to collaborate with Moscow, but to deal with a number of radical, pro-Soviet and anti-American regimes. Thus the US "flirted with radical black African governments while deemphasizing American relations with South Africa."[11] Even Cuba and Vietnam were perceived in a local or regional context rather than as local manifestations of the global competition between the superpowers. True, a number of decisionmakers (incuding National Security Adviser Zbigniew Brzezinski) did seek to reconcile the growing preoccupation with the dynamics of North-South relations, with the desire to restrain and delimit Soviet encroachment. The concept of "new influentials" in Latin America, Africa and Asia was envisaged as the link between these two foreign policy objectives. However, this attempt to integrate a residual bipolar dimension into an essentially multidimensional world view did not have much impact on the shaping of American foreign and defense policy during the period preceding the Soviet invasion of Afghanistan.

In sharp contrast with Kissinger's mitigated bipolar proclivity to contain Soviet expansionism globally through a combination of incentives and penalties, and thus to strictly delimit and constrain areas and issues of superpower collaboration until some time in the distant future, Carter's strongly-held conviction that the fear of communism was excessive, and that a posture of superpower accommodation could well be implemented in the immediate future, a priori set new parameters within which regional collaboration between Washington and Moscow could take place. Whereas in the mitigated bipolar-confrontational orientation, the parameters for collaboration in such locales of disputed high interest symmetry as the Middle East were narrow in the extreme (confining cooperation to a limited, ad hoc search for crisis-management techniques), the intrinsic nature of the multipolar-accommodative approach was compatible with a considerably wider definition of the scope of a collaborative posture. Indeed, with "the unifying threat of conflict with the Soviet Union [becoming] less intensive," and with the emergence of "a benign interpretation of the Soviets and their proxies in the Middle East and Africa," the stage was set for the Carter entourage either to ignore various forms of indirect Soviet encroachment or — in the Middle East — to embark upon an ambitious collaborative drive, designed to engage the Soviets in the search for regional accommodation to the protracted Arab-Israeli predicament.[12]

In other words, in the multipolar-accommodative world view, a narrow, minimalistic definition of the parameters of American national security was compatible with a desire to broaden the parameters of superpower collaboration in third area conflicts. It is to the analysis of this collaborative initiative as it unfolded in the Middle East in 1977, that we now turn.

Application: Carter's Collaborative Diplomatic Initiative of 1977

Kissinger's exclusionist approach of incremental change envisaged the road to peace as a protracted learning process, with the parties moving slowly and incrementally away from irreconcilable perceptions. In contrast, Carter's decisionmaking unit was committed to a considerably more optimistic view regarding the human capacity to break away rapidly from strongly-held convictions, and was predisposed to perceive peace as a single event, to be accomplished through one conference or one single document. More specifically, Kissinger tended to assign to the Geneva Peace Conference a strictly symbolic, nominal role of formally ratifying agreements negotiated unilaterally by the US. He was convinced that an entanglement at Geneva could only aggravate a situation already permeated with suspicion; the Kremlin, fully supportive of the radical Arab position, would seek above all "to restrict our freedom of action...and to shift the onus for [a deadlock] onto our shoulders."[13] By comparison, the Carter entourage — adhering to a far less ominous perception of the Soviet Union — felt that a collaborative multilateral peace effort at Geneva could catalyze a dynamic of conflict reduction and attitude change, with the Soviet Union "encouraged and put in the position of having to play a constructive role."[14]

Thus convinced that long-standing tensions could be quickly alleviated as a result of a vigorous diplomatic effort (and believing that the step-by-step approach had exhausted its potential for conflict reduction), President Carter embarked, in January 1977, upon a systematic collaborative diplomatic effort designed to revive the "Geneva option" before the end of that year. Whereas Kissinger had been committed to a minimalistic definition of the Geneva framework as a facade "for an essentially bilateral diplomacy" under American auspices,"[15] leading members of Carter's foreign policy elite, and in particular Secretary of State Vance, reiterated their determination "to stay in close touch with the Soviet Union as a co-chairman of the Geneva conference"[16] and thus to pursue a course of "continuing consultations, not just to ratify final agreements."[17] The formal and nominal was thus transformed into a real, material posture of seeking "to engage the Soviets on the most constructive basis' in the hope of thereby "[putting] them in the framework of moderation."[18]

For all the fundamental differences in orientation which separate Carter's collaborative Middle East posture from the exclusionist outlook of his predecessors, one of Kissinger's major premises evidently was integrated into Carter's system of beliefs, albeit on a different level and in a markedly different form. As has already been indicated, in pursuing his global posture of mitigated containment Kissinger was prepared to integrate a wide range of incentives into an essentially competitive framework. Such incentives, he surmised, would "give the Soviets a stake in cooperation" and thus encourage them to act with restraint.[19] However, this perception of "self containment" or of "containment by inducements,"[20] which was predicated on the expectation that the Soviet rival would "develop a self-interest in fostering the entire process of relaxation and tensions"[21] was never applied to locales of disputed high interest symmetry for the US and the Soviet Union like the Middle East, where both superpowers were engaged in fierce competition for influence.

Contrary to this propensity to restrict and confine the use of incentives to either economic or peripheral political questions, the Carter entourage was prepared to embark on an accommodative course in such "core areas" as the Middle East: "The Soviet Union," argued candidate Carter's adviser Zbigniew Brzezinski in June 1976, "has the power to complicate, to an enormous extent, the process of first obtaining and then consolidating and finally maintaining a [Middle East] settlement." That is why, he maintained, it would have to be drawn at least indirectly into the framework of a Middle East settlement. "If the Soviet Union is entirely excluded [from the peacemaking process], then it will have an additional incentive to exploit the most radical and the most extreme Arab elements as a tool of its own policy and in order to create that tension and instability in the region from which it might hope to benefit."[22]

Brzezinski's views regarding the Soviet role in the peacemaking process were fully shared by another senior member of the Carter entourage, Secretary of State Vance. Prior to his appointment as secretary of state, in May 1976, Vance maintained that "in the long run...any ultimate settlement in the Middle East is going to require some participation and cooperation from the Soviet Union." Similarly, in a private memorandum to Carter in October 1976 Vance insisted on the need to enlist the aid of the Soviet Union "at the appropriate time." "If [the Soviets] are not included," he further elaborated, "they could become a spoiler."[23]

Thus the Carter foreign policy elite, hoping that Soviet engagement in the quest for comprehensive peace would guarantee Moscow's restraint and prevent it from pursuing a recalcitrant approach, sought to proceed rapidly toward multilateral peace negotiations at Geneva. This necessarily entailed a readiness to accommodate at least some of Moscow's perceptions of the components and parameters of comprehensive peace. Most significant in this respect was Carter's de facto advocacy of the "PLO option" — a posture originally derived from his regionalist propensity to deal with radical and anti-American movements and regimes.[24] This fully coincided with the consistent Soviet demand that "some form of Palestinian entity" be established and that the PLO be recognized as the sole legitimate representative of the Arab people of Palestine (the standard Soviet terminology referred alternatively to "the right of the Palestinian Arab people to create their own state" and to "the inalienable rights of the Arab people of Palestine to self-determination"[25]). In sharp contradiction to Kissinger's tendency to delay consideration of the Palestinian predicament and to concentrate instead on areas of mutual interest, President Carter and his foreign policy advisers repeatedly stressed that the Palestinian problem would have to be put forward on a priority basis at the Geneva Peace Conference which they hoped to reconvene in 1977.[26] On April 8, 1977, for example, the president argued that the Palestinians "must be represented by a surrogate or by [themselves] directly" at the Geneva Conference, and on May 12 he asserted that there could not be "any reasonable hope for settlement of the Middle East question...without a homeland for the Palestinians."[27]

However, this initial attempt to adapt the US posture in the Palestinian sphere to some of the basic premises of Soviet diplomacy still did not provide the necessary impetus for an early resumption of the Geneva negotiations. American diplomacy simply could not overcome the strong disinclination of some of the local actors to comply. In other words, although a sufficient measure of understanding regarding the shaping of a settlement emerged on the superpower level, this global convergence of interests around an early resumption of the Geneva negotiations with some form of PLO participation, could not necessarily be implemented on the regional scene. In the first place, in the summer of 1977 the PLO refused to endorse even a modified

48

formula (with a qualifier concerning Palestinian rights) of UN Resolutions 242 and 338, which the Carter administration was prepared to regard as the equivalent of recognition of Israel's right to exist. Carter was prepared to deviate from the September 1975 American commitment to Israel (which made recognition of the PLO contingent upon the organization's acceptance of Israel's right to exist as well as Resolutions 242 and 338) and "to immediately commence plans" to talk to the PLO "if the Palestinians should [recognize] 242 in its entirety but [demand] an additional status other than just refugees." Yet the PLO, under pressure from Syria, reiterated its opposition to Resolution 242.[28] A position paper which the PLO submitted on September 18 — through Syrian Foreign Minister Abd al-Halim Khaddam to the American ambassador in Damascus — clearly indicated that the PLO remained categorically opposed to at least some of the premises incorporated in Resolution 242, and insisted on an explicit American commitment to the idea of a "national homeland for the Palestinian people" controlled by the PLO as a prerequisite to its participation in the peacemaking process.[29] Several days later the American intermediary Landrum Bolling, who knew PLO leader Yasir Arafat and was trusted by Carter, similarly reported to Brzezinski that the PLO could not accept even a modified version of Resolution 242, "unless the United States would guarantee that a Palestinian state would result from the negotiations and that the PLO would head the state."[30] This development keenly disappointed President Carter and Secretary Vance who, in July 1977, had been led by Saudi officials to believe that a significant change in the PLO position on Resolution 242 was imminent.[31]

Whether or not the administration was prepared to negotiate with the PLO, it was still confronted with an adamant Israeli refusal to accept PLO representation at Geneva or to deal with the PLO in any shape or form. Israeli leaders, and in particular Prime Minister Begin, were motivated by a highly threatening perception of the PLO as a movement seeking to destroy the State of Israel, and feared that any negotiations with the PLO were bound to involve the question of a Palestinian state on the West Bank, which they saw as a launching ground for future PLO aggression. The Israeli approach toward the PLO was most clearly demonstrated on August 9, 1977, in the course of a meeting in Jerusalem between Begin and Vance. The Israeli prime minister compared Vance's offer to negotiate with the PLO if it accepted Resolution 242, to

Neville Chamberlain's appeasement of Hitler, and added that it was a sad day for free men when the United States agreed to talk to an organization that was fully determined to annihilate the State of Israel.[32]

It is against the backdrop of this continued impasse over the question of Palestinian representation that Carter's policymakers implemented their alternative plan for superpower cooperation in the Arab-Israeli sphere. Seeking to confront the parties "with a unified Soviet-American position," on October 1, 1977 the administration released the text of a joint superpower declaration concerning the parameters of a comprehensive Middle East settlement.[33] While the exact timing of this superpower initiative undoubtedly reflected Washington's specific disenchantment with the regional constraints which threatened to disrupt its peace drive, the very notion of such a move was actually discussed for the first time in the course of a meeting held secretly in Geneva on May 19, 1977 between Vance and Gromyko. Three months later, on August 29, the possibility of a joint superpower statement on the principles of a Middle East settlement was raised once again during a meeting in Washington between Secretary Vance and Soviet Ambassador to the US Anatoly Dobrynin. Convinced that "it made sense to start bringing the Soviets carefully into the process of preparing for a Geneva conference of which they would be one of the co-chairmen," Vance discussed with Dobrynin, during a meeting held on September 9, a draft text of the statement. The final text of the document was developed in the course of a lengthy session between Vance and Gromyko on September 30.[34]

The October 1 initiative proceeded far beyond the limited parameters of superpower collaboration as outlined in the mitigated bipolar-confrontational approach. It incorporated maximalistic elements of a superpower condominium strategy, one which is "geared toward jointly imposing on weaker states terms for conflict resolution that the superpowers have worked out on their own."[35] This attempt to implement in the region a posture predicated on a collusive condominium strategy was based on the multipolar-accommodative assumption that the collaborative elements in the American-Soviet dyad outweighed the competitive components. Whereas the mitigated version of the bipolar-confrontational orientation as implemented by Nixon and Kissinger ruled out the short-term possibility of superpower collaboration of such proportions (though hoping that, in time, "the new positive relationship with the Soviet Union would become part of a new, more stable international system"[36]), the multipolar-accommodative approach was based on the assumption that this era of "new positive relationship" had already emerged, and that, therefore, both powers could now jointly exercise control "in a limited sphere or over particular issues as a step toward a more general management of the affairs of the world."[37]

This complex of basic and general multipolar-accommodative notions from which the October 1 initiative was derived, was further reinforced by a set of more concrete and expedient assumptions. Central among these was the belief, articulated by Brzezinski as early as the summer of 1975, that a powerful demonstration of superpower unity was the optimal means for signaling resolve and credibility, and was therefore bound to put effective "pressure on the Arabs and Israelis, especially if...endorsed by Western Europe and Japan." It was expected that "a public US posture in favor of such a settlement would probably gain both domestic and international support."[38] Israel, confronted with this fait accompli and faced with a determined American approach, would be unwilling to risk a confrontation which entailed the prospects of growing isolation and considerable hardship, and would be forced to attend the Geneva Conference on the terms specified in the statement.

One year later, candidate Carter expressed similar notions regarding the desirability of a joint superpower initiative for resolving the Arab-Israeli predicament. "It may be that...in the future, after unpublicized negotiations between us and the Soviet Union, we might jointly make a public proposal of a solution to the Middle East....The Soviet Union is going to have to participate in a forceful way before Syria will be amenable to any productive negotiations with Israel."[39]

Ultimately, faced with a continued deadlock over the question of Palestinian representation, the administration set out to implement its "superpower option" in order to coerce Israel into modifying its Palestinian posture.[40] Convinced that "we are not just an idle bystander [or] uninterested intermediary or mediator,"[41] and that the United States had "the legitimate right to exercise its own leverage,"[42] Carter and Brzezinski thus converted into a concrete posture their preexisting notion of superpower collaboration as an effective means of promoting a Middle East settlement. President Carter's words (*Time*, August 8, 1977) most explicitly expose this scenario:

> I think that if a particular leader of one of the countries should find that his position is in direct contravention to the position of all the parties involved *including ourselves and the Soviet Union,* and was a narrowly defined question in his own country, *there would be a great impetus on that leader to conform with the overwhelming opinion*[43]

Thus a circle had been closed in American Middle East policy. Kissinger's unilateral approach (derived from his mitigated bipolar world view) of de facto excluding the Soviets from the peacemaking process — while maintaining a facade of sporadic consultations with Soviet Foreign Minister Gromyko, as well as of repeated reassurances of future participation — was abandoned by Carter's collaborative course, which was predicated on the premises of an accommodative vision of the world. In the Middle East, this posture culminated in the drive to consolidate a superpower condominium as a means of defusing the Arab-Israel predicament.

Thus, whereas the representatives of the mitigated bipolar confrontational orientation consistently refused any superpower trade-off involving "core" issues and interests in such areas of disputed high-interest symmetry as the Middle East, the architects of the multipolar-accommodative outlook were prepared to subordinate their competitive interests to what was perceived as the more pressing need to elicit Soviet cooperation in order to promote stability in all parts of the international system.

The US also was predisposed to assign priority to the goal of forging a superpower coalition at the expense of straining relations with local disputants. Thus, although it had agreed in its September 1975 Memorandum of Understanding with Israel that the participation at Geneva "of any possible additional state, group or organization will require the agreement of all the initial participants," the joint superpower statement of October 1, 1977 openly called for the inclusion of representatives of the "Palestinian people" in the Geneva peace forum. The document asserted:

> Both governments are convinced that vital interests of the peoples of this area, as well as the interests of strengthening peace and international security in general, urgently dictate the necessity of achieving, as soon as possible, a just and lasting settlement of the Arab-Israeli conflict. This settlement should be comprehensive, incorporating all parties

concerned and all questions. The United States and the Soviet Union believe that, within the framework of a comprehensive settlement of the Middle East problem, all specific questions of the settlement should be resolved, including such key issues as withdrawal of Israeli Armed Forces from territories occupied in the 1967 conflict [and] *the resolution of the Palestinian question, including ensuring the legitimate rights of the Palestinian people.*

...The United States and the Soviet Union believe that the only right and effective way for achieving a fundamental solution to all aspects of Middle East problem in its entirety is negotiations within the framework of the Geneva Peace Conference, specially convened for these purposes, with participation in its work of the representatives of all the parties involved in the conflict including those of the Palestinian people, and legal and contractual formalization of the decisions reached at the conference. In their capacity as co-chairmen of the Geneva conference, the United States and the USSR affirm their intention, through joint efforts and in their contacts with the parties concerned, to facilitate in every way the resumption of the work of the conference not later than December 1977.[44]

In view of Carter's repeated references to the PLO as an organization which "represents, certainly, a substantial part of the Palestinians," there could be no doubt that the two superpowers sought to include the PLO in the Geneva Conference.[45] Furthermore, as Spiegel points out, in this document the United States "accepted for the first time the phrase *legitimate rights of the Palestinian people,* once viewed as an Arab code for displacing Israel with a Palestinian state"[46] (the administration had previously used the term *interests* rather than rights).

Moreover, notwithstanding Washington's 1975 commitment to Israel "to consult fully and seek to concert its position and strategy at the Geneva Peace Conference on this issue with the Government of Israel," the October 1 initiative was not preceded by any form of notification (let alone of consultations with Jerusalem), and thus completely surprised Israel's decisionmakers.[47] Finally, as Cohen points out, absent from the document "were key formulas in the rules of the game between Israel and the United States." Specifically, there was no reference in the joint declaration to US Resolutions 242 and 338, despite the fact that the US government had repeatedly affirmed that these resolutions consituted the sole basis for the convening of the Geneva Conference. Thus the administration, finding it impossible to entice the PLO into accepting a modified version of Resolution 242, opted to bypass the exact terms of its commitment to the Resolution with the publication of a declaration not under UN auspices.[48]

Carter's willingness to decouple the Middle East predicament from the global superpower competition had thus precipitated a strategy intended to utilize Moscow as an additional coercive leverage on some of the local parties. In other words, while committed to an essentially accommodative global posture, the Carter policy elite resorted, in October 1977, to a coercive strategy vis-à-vis its regional allies, and primarily Israel.

That this strategy failed abjectly was due to both the projected superpower partner — the USSR — and the local partners who were to be coerced. For one, the expectation that Moscow would "follow along and take advantage of any constructive step toward peace" did not materialize. The initial hope of consolidating a "useful and constructive connection" between the superpowers gradually evaporated during subsequent months, until — in the aftermath of the Soviet invasion of Afghanistan — it was formally abandoned by a frustrated, disillusioned administration.[49]

Secondly, though declaratively at least, Moscow readily supported the Carter initiative — it not only guaranteed the Soviets a central role in the peacemaking process but accorded with their basic approach on the Palestinian front — the attempt to coerce the local parties, and especially Israel, into accepting the new formula as a fait accompli, was abortive. While the bipolar-confrontational policy orientation by definition precludes the possibility of superpower collaboration reaching the level of a condominium (which implies a willingness to subordinate competitive interests for the sake of jointly and forcefully defusing a dispute), the multipolar-accommodative readiness of the Carter entourage to proceed beyond the narrow, Kissingerian parameters of collaboration in the Middle East could not alone guarantee that the concept of superpower condominium, as embedded in the October 1 statement, would be translated into reality. In other words, for all its significance as a necessary condition, the existence of some compatibility in the definition of interests or parameters of a settlement does not in itself constitute a sufficient condition for the effective pursuit of any form of a superpower condominium strategy. As was the case in the wake of the October 1 declaration, a highly asymmetrical regional setting, whose major actors remained adamantly and irrevocably opposed to the superpower initiative, proved to be the dominant force which ultimately foiled the entire design, forcing Washington to reconsider its priorities and predilections in the Arab-Israeli arena.

In the context of the American-Israeli dyad, the very fact that the two superpowers had decided to embark on a collaborative course without prior consultation with Jerusalem, was interpreted by several prominent members of Israel's high policy elite, including Acting Prime Minister Simcha Ehrlich, as the "first signs of the superpowers' desire to impose a settlement." Ehrlich, voicing a widely held view, accused Washington of trying "to improve its relations with the Soviets at Israel's expense." A period of national emergency might lie ahead, he predicted, and Israel's stamina under pressure would depend primarily on the spiritual strength of its people and on the support of American and world Jewry.[50] Beyond this widespread Israeli perception that the US had violated the rules of the game governing its relations with Israel, and particularly those concerning peace negotiations, Israel's policymakers charged that the communique contained the seeds of a Palestinian state, and that it implied PLO participation at Geneva. "Under no condition," Ehrlich warned, "will we sit with the PLO."[51]

Indeed, the entire issue of PLO participation in the peacemaking process had long been perceived in Jerusalem as a "core" or cardinal question pertaining to Israel's survival. This made Israel resolute and irreconcilable in its opposition to the new initiative, and overshadowed the fear of an open confrontation with Washington.[52] In George's terminology: the disutility of the action demanded (the de facto recognition of the PLO) far exceeded, in Israel's eyes, the disutility of any threatening ramifications (such as the withholding of economic and military aid) which could have resulted from an intensified crisis in American-Israeli relations. The new demands upon Israel that were implied in the document could not erode Israel's motivation to cling to its initial position of total refusal to negotiate with the PLO. Given this asymmetry of motivation favoring Israel, this concerted drive to redefine the parameters of a settlement was predestined to collapse.[53]

In the face of a perceived threat to such a central tenet in Israel's security posture, there was in fact no sanction which the US could have used to coerce Israel. As Foreign Minister Dayan affirmed in the aftermath of the crisis:

> If the US insists on a Palestinian State, I think that any Israeli Government would reject it. And if we have to make the choice tomorrow of what to do — have a breach with the US...or accept a Palestinian state — we would rather have these problems with the US than agree to a Palestinian state, which we seriously think would eventually bring the destruction of Israel.[54]

Indeed, the administration's expectations that the document would eliminate the obstacles on the road to Geneva by compelling Israel to face up to the "fact" that there could be no peace without the PLO, failed to materialize.

But Israel was not the only local power that vehemently opposed the superpowers' effort to translate into reality their shared visions of regional accommodation. President Sadat of Egypt was also dismayed by the American willingness to involve the Soviets in the peacemaking process, and decided to forego, at least temporarily, American mediation and instead take the route of direct negotiations with Israel. While this keen sense of disappointment with American diplomacy was only one among several considerations that motivated Sadat to embark on his peace mission of November 1977, no doubt the timing of his initiative was largely prompted by the ill-fated superpower statement.

Sadat's initiative, which led to the Camp David accords and the conclusion, in March 1979, of a peace treaty between Egypt and Israel, was clearly incompatible with Washington's initial plan to reconvene the Geneva forum before the end of 1977. And although the administration sought, during the period immediately following Sadat's mission to Jerusalem, to redirect Egyptian policy so as to accommodate its posture of "continued cooperation" with the Soviet Union, it became clear in subsequent weeks that Washington's hopes could not be reconciled with a recalcitrant regional environment.[55]

Concurrent with Israel and Egypt's staunch opposition to the statement, the president and his advisers were confronted with a storm of domestic protest. "The Soviet-American Communique aroused extraordinary opposition to the president's policy, while draining confidence in his leadership at the precise moment when

56

the administration was mustering for the sharpest clash yet with Israel."[56] Deprived of an adequate basis of domestic support or, in George's terminology, of "policy legitimacy,"[57] the administration was quickly forced to modify its strategy and offer incentives to Israel which amounted to a tacit repudiation of several components of the declaration. The US Congress, which took a leading role in challenging the cognitive as well as moral "basis of legitimacy" of the plan,[58] reacted with defiance to the surprising initiative, with 150 congressmen expressing "grave concern" over the matter. Angry statements were issued by senators Henry Jackson, Robert Dole, Daniel Patrick Moynihan, Howard Baker, Clifford Case and Jacob Javits. Most senatorial critics were particularly incensed by what they regarded as the unwise and unnecessary invitation to the Soviet Union to reenter the scene of Middle East negotiations. In the words of Senator Jackson: "The American people must certainly raise the question of why bring the Russians in at a time when the Egyptians have been throwing them out."[59] The Jewish community's leadership reacted equally swiftly and unequivocally. The Conference of Presidents of Major Jewish Organizations, headed by Rabbi Alexander Schindler, labeled the October 1 Communique "an abandonment of America's historical commitment to the security and survival of Israel," and an avalanche of angry telephone calls and telegrams descended on the White House — mostly from aroused Jewish groups.[60] As Spiegel asserts, "not one senator or congressman rose to defend the administration, which was widely seen as catering to the Russian and Arab positions. After American officials had worked successfully for years to reduce Soviet influence over the Mideast peace process and in the area as a whole, critics could not understand why the administration had suddenly invited Moscow to return."[61]

Against the backdrop of vociferous reaction and the administration's overall inability to consolidate even a minimal basis of support — both domestic and external — for its collaborative design, the October 1 drive can indeed be regarded as "a striking example of complete political miscalculation."[62] Far from isolating Israel by mobilizing domestic and international support in favor of the joint statement, the Carter entourage found itself isolated and embattled in the wake of the storm of protest which greeted the move. Consequently, American policymakers were quickly forced to shift gears and offer Israel compensation of such magnitude as to render obsolete most aspects of the new strategy.[63] In a working paper signed on October 5, 1977, by secretaries Dayan and Vance, it was mutually agreed that UN Resolutions 242 and 338 remained the only basis for negotiations at Geneva, and that all the initial terms of reference remained in force "except as may be agreed to by the parties." Although the working paper, like the superpower declaration, called for Palestinian participation in the Geneva Conference, it explicitly reconfirmed the 1975 American position according to which "any new participant in Geneva must be agreed to by all the parties."[64]

Not only did the Carter presidency prove incapable of "organizing Geneva with the Soviets." As the months passed, it also could not remain totally oblivious to mounting indications of Soviet regional intransigence which were clearly incompatible with its preconceived multipolar-accommodative world view. In the first place, Moscow continuously attempted to discredit President Sadat and his peace initiative. It gave full support to the "rejectionist front" while attacking Washington's perceived desire to promote a separate peace between Egypt and Israel and thus "to break up Arab unity." It also accused the US of "torpedoing the Geneva Conference even before it begins."[65] Concurrently, Cuban military advisers and Soviet arms began to arrive in Ethiopia, and on November 26, 1977 the Soviets launched a massive airlift of Cuban troops and Soviet tanks and other arms, which surpassed any previous demonstration of their capacity to intervene decisively in distant places. The airlift, which drastically altered the course of the Ogaden War, lasted for six weeks. During this period, Cuba sent between 12,000 and 17,000 troops, including three combat brigades, to Ethiopia from Cuba and Angola, while the Soviet Union sent up to $1 billion worth of arms.[66]

Faced with these dramatic developments, the president gradually became more circumspect in his hopes for superpower cooperation in either the heart or the periphery of the region. As early as January 12, 1978, President Carter expressed concern about "the Soviet Union's unwarranted involvement in Africa," especially the supply of arms. This statement, however, was not coupled with any pressure designed to dissuade Moscow from continuing, directly or by proxy, to send arms and military advisers to Ethiopia.[67] Similarly, on March 24, 1978, Carter described the overall state of superpower relations in language markedly more restrained and enigmatic than his optimistic statements (such as his Notre Dame speech) of the preceding year: "Let me say I think we are at a delicate stage in our relationship with the Soviet Union. The various matters which we are dealing with...the Soviet Union are mixed....And I think we are always going to find this kind of a mix. It is a very complex set of relationships."[68] Carter's growing proclivity to deviate from the logic of the multipolar-accommodative approach and to embark instead on a new course which incorporated certain mitigated bipolar-confrontational premises, was even more clearly evident on May 12, 1978, in a presidential statement permeated with uncertainty concerning the Soviet "operational code" in third areas and the prospects for maintaining the initial strategy of decoupling regional crises from the context of East-West relations:

> I have let Brezhnev know directly from me to him...that the Soviet's continuation of intrusion into Africa, with military force, was a major obstacle to trust on the part of the American people that the Soviets want peace and want to have a successful detente effort....We let the Soviets know that although we want to have peace with them...we're not afraid of them, our military strength will be maintained, their intrusion into Africa is both unnecessary, unwarranted, and tends to convince the American people that the Soviets are not sincere in their commitment to detente and their search for peace.[69]

And although, during the period immediately following the Ethiopian airlift, some administration officials (primarily Secretary of State Vance) remained convinced that "nothing should interfere with the dialogue over the limitation of strategic arms," this non-linkage posture progressively eroded in the wake of yet another sharp increase in the number of Soviet advisers and Cuban troops in Ethiopia, which — in late 1978 — precipitated a full-fledged Ethiopian counteroffensive in the Ogaden.[70]

While Washington's immediate reaction to the Soviet march in the Horn of Africa was ineffective, the crisis further accelerated an ongoing process of reassessing Soviet global and regional intentions and policies. With the post-Vietnam syndrome gradually fading, and with a growing public recognition that "the United States was lagging behind the Soviet Union in military strength and overall influence in world affairs,"[71] the stage was set for the de facto abandonment of at least some of the accommodative premises incorporated into the administration's original vision of the international system. The administration was therefore progressively forced to adjust its preconceived beliefs to the real forces comprising "the operational environment."[72] As Garthoff notes, "one consequence of the crisis in the Horn was a general toughening of President Carter's stance toward the Soviet Union...which contributed to a general hardening of relations in 1978."[73]

Another turning point along the road back to bipolarity was the conclusion, through exclusive American mediation, of the Camp David accords in September 1978. This constituted once again a significant departure from the initial posture of superpower collaboration in the Arab-Israeli sphere. Although the administration had hoped, during the period immediately preceding Camp David, to convert Sadat's initiative into a more comprehensive peacemaking drive (with the Geneva multilateral forum as its major peace mechanism), it was largely constrained by Egypt and Israel. Seeking to exclude the Soviet Union from the diplomatic process, both local parties "joined together in a tacit coalition to force the United States to abandon its attempt at condominium with the USSR."[74] Washington's desire to "build on the momentum" created by the November 1977 breakthrough in Egyptian-Israeli relations and thus to utilize it as a springboard for accelerating the drive toward resolving the Palestinian predicament in its entirety, therefore clashed with the wish of Egypt and Israel to bypass the Geneva framework and instead to pursue bilateral negotiations under the umbrella of the newly-formed "Cairo Peace Conference."

Even here the US hoped that the Cairo meetings would "pave the way toward an ultimate Geneva Conference" and toward "the negotiation of a comprehensive peace." But it quickly became apparent that, rather than fueling an overall process of conflict reduction, Sadat's peace move was disjointed from the realities of an increasingly recalcitrant Arab world. Furthermore, the administration's insistence on the need to tackle head-on a plethora of emotion-laden issues pertaining to the future status of the West Bank as an integral part of any Egyptian-Israeli accord, only aggravated an already tense situation in American-Israeli relations.

It is against this backdrop of continued impasse that the American role in the Camp David conference must be understood. Incapable of implementing its much-desired objective of comprehensive peace (and faced with the grim prospects of an imminent collapse of the entire negotiating process), the Carter foreign policy unit was ultimately compelled to deviate from its initial vision of regional accommodation and a collaborative strategy, and to adopt instead an exclusionist posture advocating a separate peace between Egypt and Israel. It was further influenced in this direction by such adverse developments as the rapidly intensifying Iranian crisis and continued turbulence and instability in Turkey — trends that encouraged the president to build and consolidate any islands of stability that might function as a bulwark against the militant forces of encroachment and radicalization. The emerging strategy, which was closely patterned on the notions of unilateralism and incrementalism, bore a striking resemblance to an entire cluster of Kissingerian premises and notions. For just as Kissinger was consistently predisposed to concentrate first on areas of mutual interest and to sidestep emotion-laden issues, so did Carter agree at Camp David to postpone consideration of such difficult questions as Jerusalem, and to segment complex issues into individual elements which could be negotiated separately. Moreover, the administration adopted Kissinger's belief that in order to defuse the multifaceted Arab-Israeli conflict, it was necessary to proceed gradually until all the parties were emotionally prepared to abandon confrontational ideologies and irreconcilable dogmas for the sake of adopting a more accommodative approach.

American Camp David diplomacy also deviated from Carter's previous insistence on Soviet involvement in the peacemaking process. In view of Moscow's intensive involvement in the Ogaden War and its persistent support for the Arab Rejectionist Front, any remaining hopes of reconciling the notion of superpower collaboration in the Middle East with harsh regional realities finally evaporated. As a result, the Carter foreign policy machinery came around to support, at Camp David, the Kissingerian concept of exclusive American mediation which, in the not too distant past, had been alien to its multipolar-accommodative thinking. At Camp David, Carter mediated

a comprehensive and specific settlement of all outstanding political and military issues between Egypt and Israel, along with a very general and imprecise framework on the political future of the Palestinian people. Although the agreement was comprehensive between Egypt and Israel, it was partial and limited in all other respects, couched in vague language which enabled each side to interpret the concept of "autonomy" for the Palestinians as they saw fit. The president achieved agreement only by resorting to deliberately imprecise language to mask disagreement, by postponing issues that were impossible to resolve, and ultimately by agreeing to disagree on such matters as the status of Jerusalem...Carter's work looked remarkably like that of Kissinger.[75]

Indeed, an analysis of the twofold Camp David framework clearly indicates that only one document emerging from the summit, namely, the Egyptian-Israeli accord, was drafted as a short-term, operational agreement. Not only is the second Camp David agreement, which outlines the parameters of a West Bank settlement, fraught with ambiguities, but it is only loosely linked to the Egyptian-Israeli accord. In other words: nowhere in the entire Camp David record is there any indication that the two agreements are contingent upon one another, that implementation of the Egyptian-Israeli accord is dependent upon progress in the West Bank.

Spiegel concludes:

> Carter thus expressed the anomaly of his administration's Middle East record. At each juncture it had sought a comprehensive settlement only to be thwarted by Arab disputes, other Arabs' hostility to the Sadat peace initiative, and Israeli fears that Egyptian-Israeli agreements would founder on the Palestinian issue. Carter had been forced to choose the possible immediate step instead of the preferable comprehensive approach. The notion of a Geneva Conference had been replaced by an Egyptian-Israeli initiative; at Camp David, comprehensiveness had been subordinated to the Egyptian-Israeli arena. In the [peace] treaty negotiations, the same process had started again, with the focus on linkage and an autonomy timetable giving way to vague formulations accommodating Israeli fears.[76]

In the aftermath of Camp David, Soviet officials strongly criticized American summit diplomacy for seeking, according to Soviet leader Leonid Brezhnev, "to split the Arab countries." "The road of separate talks and concessions to the aggressor," warned Brezhnev on October 5, 1978, "does not bring peace any closer."[77] Thus as 1978 approached its end, it became evident that the gap separating the respective policies and objectives of the superpowers in the Middle East could not be bridged. In this respect, the events which were to unfold in 1979 merely aggravated an already tense situation. Indeed, the conclusion, in March 1979, of the peace treaty between Egypt and Israel incensed Moscow, which reiterated its support for the Arab rejectionist camp.

With its benign, highly optimistic multipolar-accommodative visions receding rapidly into the background, the Carter administration saw the Soviet invasion of Afghanistan, in December 1979, as a watershed or "trigger event" that transformed its residual bipolar-confrontational attitudes into a manifest, dominant foreign policy orientation.[78] Coming in the wake of a series of Soviet proxy military interventions, the Afghanistan invasion convinced the architects of American foreign policy that Soviet behavior formed a pattern of expansion and aggrandizement inconsistent with the spirit of detente.

Viewed in this context, "the vigor of the American reaction cannot be attributed to the Soviet invasion alone." As Garthoff further notes, although the move into Afghanistan was perceived "as both an affront and a potential threat, even more important was that it triggered the release of tensions that had been growing in Soviet-American relations over Angola, Ethiopia, Shaba, the Yemens, Cambodia, and, most recently, the brigade in Cuba....Afghanistan provided a focus and crystallized the consensus that the United States must do something."[79]

In much the same way that the traumatic experiences of Vietnam and Watergate constituted the trigger events which precipitated the momentary decline of "the Pearl Harbor paradigm," so did the Afghanistan invasion comprise yet another turning point in the course of American foreign policy, albeit in the opposite direction. In the words of Brzezinski, who describes in his memoirs the administration's immediate reaction to the Afghan invasion: "We all knew that a major watershed had been reached in the American-Soviet relationship."[80] President Carter's personal reaction clearly illustrates the profound impact which the Afghanistan crisis had upon his "background images" of the Soviet Union. In a television interview on December 31, 1979, the president stated that "this action of the Soviets has made a more dramatic change in my own opinion of what the Soviets' ultimate goals are than anything they've done in the previous time I've been in office."[81]

In the aftermath of the Afghan invasion, the Carter administration did remain committed to a number of multipolar-accommodative premises. But now it was clearly motivated by a highly menacing bipolar perception of an ambitious adversary, seeking to gain control of the Persian Gulf region. Contrary to its pre-Afghanistan predisposition to deemphasize or obfuscate the parameters of East-West relations, the administration in early 1980 moved toward adopting a new posture of containment, "the Carter Doctrine," which was intended to prevent any major disruption in the global (and regional) balance of power.

As Strobe Talbott observes:

> Like most incoming administrations, the Carter administration had been determined to preside over a breakthrough in Soviet-American relations...Carter and Brzezinski had vowed [initially] to relegate Soviet-American relations to a less central position in the scheme of US foreign policy. They criticized their predecessors, particularly former Secretary of State Henry Kissinger, for allowing their attempts at management of the superpower relationship to obscure, distort or altogether prevent consideration of other issues: trilateral ties with Western Europe and Japan, the North-South dialogue, the evolution of a new economic order, and the search for peaceful settlement geared to local needs rather than geopolitical goals....Carter and Brzezinski...wanted to distance themselves from the we/they, East/West view of the world that marked, in different ways, Dean Acheson's containment, John Foster Dulles' brinkmanship and Henry Kissinger's realpolitik....By the end of 1979, those hopes of three years before echoed with a distinctly futile and even unrealistic ring. Deemphasizing the Soviet-American relationship necessarily meant injecting it with a new degree of stability, if not placidity. Yet just the opposite had occurred: the relationship had deteriorated....The impulse to build bridges to Havana and Hanoi was moribund, a casualty of continuing Cuban adventurism in Africa and the Vietnamese occupation of Cambodia. By the autumn of 1979, Carter and Brzezinski were no longer calling the Cubans just "proxies" of the Soviet Union: they were calling them "puppets." In short, by the end of 1979, the United States was more preoccupied than ever with the problem of how to deal with the Russians.[82]

In progressively moving from the pole of superpower accommodation to the extreme of confrontation and containment, the Carter foreign policy elite clearly reflected the changing mood of

American public opinion:

In September 1979, for the first time since 1960, more Americans (38 percent) supported a defense increase as against maintaining the current level (36 percent) or a decrease (16 percent). By December 1979, before the invasion of Afghanistan, 51 percent of the public favored an increase, 31 percent the current level, and 9 percent a decrease....Initial public support for Carter's post-Afghanistan sanctions against the Soviet Union was overwhelming, and in general during 1980...the public maintained...a fiercely hawkish mood.[83]

In the words of Bruce Russet and Donald Deluca: "It is now [in 1981] clear that public opinion has again shifted, back toward a much more assertive, or hawkish, posture in world affairs, toward a widespread determination to rebuild American military capabilities and to reaffirm a readiness to use those capabilities in defense of perceived interests."[84]

The search for bases in such locations as Somalia, Kenya, Oman and Egypt, the intensified drive "to further enhance the capacity of rapid deployment forces to protect our interests," and the imposition of economic and political sanctions on the Soviet Union — these were the major tenets of the new posture. During the period immediately following the invasion, it incorporated both accommodative elements (such as the desire to improve relations with several anti-American regimes) and mitigated bipolar-confrontational components.[85] It combined "punitive sanctions, a freeze on American-Soviet relations, increasing geopolitical leverage (especially through the new relationship with China), and building regional geopolitical positions of strength (the Carter Doctrine)."[86]

True, the version of bipolarity articulated by such high-ranking administration officials as Secretary of Defense Harold Brown during the post-invasion period appears subdued when juxtaposed with the images of the world which shaped the thinking of "classical" pure representatives of the bipolar-confrontational orientation like James Forrestal or Walt Rostow (and which were later to shape the initial thinking of the Reagan foreign policy elite). Notwithstanding the differences, it is clear that the strategy recommended by a near-consensus of Carter's foreign policy elite during most of 1980 was predicated on the premises of confrontational bipolarity. While Secretary of State Vance was an exception to this rule, even his own subordinates were not:

> Ever since the end of the Second World War, the most dangerous factor in world politics has been the competition between the United States and the Soviet Union....The Soviet challenge is a broad one. It involves ideological, economic, and military challenges to Western ideals, to Western political and economic systems, and to Western security....The critical factor in curbing Soviet military power...is not what we do now but whether we are prepared to be firm and principled during the next decade....Adversaries abroad...act more rationally, and thus less dangerously, when they see clearly that US policies are articulated coherently and consistently.[87]

By January 8, 1980, Carter was predisposed to couple the Afghanistan crisis with the global balance of power, and thus to adopt — at least on the rhetorical level — the very essence of the bipolar-confrontational approach:

> In my own opinion...the Soviet invasion of Afghanistan is the greatest threat to peace since the Second World War. It's a sharp escalation in the aggressive history of the Soviet Union....We are the other superpower on Earth, and it became my responsibility...to take action that would prevent the Soviets from this invasion with impunity. The Soviets had to suffer the consequences. *In my judgment, our own Nation's security was directly threatened. There is no doubt that the Soviets' move into Afghanistan, if done without adverse consequences, would have resulted in the temptation to move again and again until they reached warm water ports or until they acquired control over a major portion of the world's oil supplies.*[88]

In this respect, the fourth and last year of the Carter administration can be regarded as "a precursor to the Reagan turn toward confrontation....In many ways January 1980 was a sharper turning point than January 1981, when Ronald Reagan was inaugurated and repudiated detente."[89] After an interlude of three years, the bipolar-confrontational paradigm — which, in various forms, had been the predominant policy orientation for more than three decades — was reinstated as the focal point of American diplomacy. As we have already witnessed, it was to dictate an increasingly irreconcilable global posture during most of President Reagan's first term in the White House.

Chapter 4. The Limits of Superpower Collaboration: Hindsight and Foresight

The preceding pages did not attempt a chronological historical review of the search for superpower settlement of the Arab-Israeli conflict as it has unfolded since the Yom Kippur War. Instead, our analysis of divergent foreign policy orientations which at times generated specific policies for defusing the Middle East predicament, sought primarily to identify the parameters within which American peacemaking diplomacy was likely to evolve. On the basis of this analysis, it is possible to isolate two dichotomous trends regarding superpower collaboration in the Arab-Israeli sphere.

The first is a minimalist form of collaboration, which is associated with the mitigated bipolar-confrontational outlook (the pure variant of this approach rules out the possibility of almost any collaboration, being predicated on the principles of challenge, rollback or containment). While fully compatible with a wide range of crisis-management and crisis-avoidance techniques, this category is strictly confined — at least in locales of disputed high interest symmetry such as the Middle East — to procedures "that keep open lines of communication or seek to prevent...misunderstandings,"[1] or to merely symbolic forms of superpower collaboration.

In the case of Kissinger's diplomatic drive during the period immediately following the Yom Kippur War (as well as in the case of Robert Anderson's peace mission of 1955), the specific nature of the exclusionist strategy which derived from the mitigated bipolar-confrontational approach approximated a model of incremental, step-by-step progress. In other instances, such as the Reagan Peace Plan of September 1, 1982, the way in which these unilateralist principles were implemented incorporated the premises of the comprehensive method.

The second trend is of a maximilistic nature. Derived from the premises of the multipolar-accommodative perspective, it is compatible with far more comprehensive and ambitious strategies of collaboration, ranging from the development of multilateral forums for conflict resolution or amelioration, to the establishment of a superpower condominium.

The concept of a superpower condominium entails "a high degree of collaboration in an effort by the superpowers to maintain order in the system, and to subordinate their competitive interests and the interests of their allies to this goal." In theory, a condominium strategy can exceed the level of mere policy coordination. As Snyder further notes, the maximalistic variant of this strategy incorporates coercive elements, with the two dominant powers jointly "policing" weaker allies or client states into acceptance of certain terms for conflict resolution that the superpowers have worked out on their own.[2]

A collaborative peace strategy, derived from the premises of the multipolar-accommodative orientation, can be pursued in either a comprehensive or an incremental fashion. In the case of Carter's 1977 diplomatic initiative, superpower collaboration was expected to provide the impetus for a rapid comprehensive settlement. In theory, however (and in various related nongovernmental peace proposals such as the Brookings Plan), a collaborative peace initiative may be pursued or implemented incrementally.

Having defined two basic modes of superpower collaboration, several remarks are in order regarding their applicability in the Middle East. For one, the more ambitious and comprehensive the nature of the collaborative strategy pursued, the more likely it is to encounter opposition from at least some of the local protagonists. As Stein points out, the historical record of the Arab-Israeli conflict shows that "every attempt at a comprehensive solution, negotiated simultaneously among all the parties, did not succeed." Even when the environment was conducive, as during the Carter presidency, a comprehensive strategy of collaboration invariably failed. In contrast, any progress that has been made toward mitigating the dispute has been incremental, gradual, and bilateral. Given the intensity and durability of the conflict, only a phased step-by-step strategy has permitted the parties to reduce the risks of concessions. Thus, no matter how logical and tidy the comprehensive solution is, "a bargaining process which encourages modest concessions in the initial phases, builds in incentives for larger concessions over time, and carefully structures transitional arrangements, seems far more likely to succeed in reducing an intractable conflict."[3]

Against this backdrop of cumulative experience, it is not unreasonable to hypothesize that the concept of negotiating interim and transitional arrangements (for example, between Israel and Jordan), while deferring final settlement issues, has better prospects of implementation than the comprehensive approach of seeking peace under the auspices of an international conference — unless, as was the case in 1973, the international framework is but a springboard for bilateral negotiations.

A second broad observation would indicate that, while an elucidation of the cognitive sources of American thinking and behavior in approaching the Arab-Israel dispute could help determine the parameters of certain derivative strategies, a mere understanding of Washington's cognitive map and operational code cannot be regarded as a magic formula for accurately predicting specific policy lines and initiatives. As has already been pointed out, cognitive perspectives and beliefs do not constitute "a set of rules that are applied mechanically by policymakers when they make a decision."[4] Nor are these perceptions immune to change and modification, precipitated by the dynamic nature of the "operational environment." Indeed, none of the peace strategies which were patterned on the premises of either confrontational bipolarity or accommodative multipolarity could have remained intact when challenged by a defiant reality. Thus President Reagan's initial pure bipolar-confrontational approach gradually became susceptible to certain mitigated premises both on the global and the regional levels. In Huntington's words: "By 1982 signs existed that the hostility wave [toward the Soviet Union]...now might be starting to recede....The Reagan administration tended to be drawn leftward to a more moderate position."[5] In the Middle Eastern theater this willingness to set aside certain preconceived irreconcilable images of the Soviet adversary eventually became evident in the superpower discussions on crisis avoidance held in Vienna in February 1985, in Geneva in November 1985, and in Stockholm in July 1986. A new American sensitivity to the "operational environment" was similarly manifested on May 31, 1985, when Secretary of State Shultz implicitly abandoned the administration's initial posture of categorical rejection of the very notion of an international conference as an appropriate peacemaking device. Instead, he formulated a number of preconditions for convening the forum, including demands that Moscow relax its immigration policy and curb antisemitism.[6]

Similarly, when Kissinger's exclusionist diplomacy, derived from his mitigated bipolar-confrontational perspective, failed to generate an on-going dynamic during the months which followed the conclusion of the Sinai Interim Agreement of September 1975, the secretary himself suggested that it be supplemented by collaborative techniques to avert a prolonged impasse in the process of political accommodation. The "Saunders document" of November 12, 1975, which alluded to the Palestinian dimension of the Arab-Israeli conflict as being, in many ways, the "heart of the conflict," should be viewed against the backdrop of this growing sense of disillusionment with the inability of the American exclusionist approach to create new opportunities for the future and thus accelerate the process of peace. Indeed, by 1976 Kissinger's vaunted shuttle diplomacy, which was closely patterned on the principle of unilateralism, had stalled. Any major steps in 1976, maintains Spiegel, "were difficult because of (1) the election campaign and the President's bitter primary struggle with Ronald Reagan, (2) Kissinger's controversial position — attacked by both the Republican right and the Democratic left, and (3) the Lebanese civil war that stole Arab attention."[7]

Finally, President Carter was also compelled to shift gears. Three years after setting out to translate his multipolar-accommodative vision of peace into a new reality, he adopted a global and regional course which incorporated an entire new complex of bipolar-confrontational premises.

Notwithstanding this tendency toward vacillation and fluctuation in the American peacemaking posture, one conclusion is clear. A strategy of superpower collaboration for defusing the Arab-Israeli conflict, of the kind that the Carter entourage sought to promote, requires for its effective implementation that two clusters of constraints — one domestic and the other external — be met. In the first place, the forces of public opinion, Congress, the media and powerful interest groups must lend their support to the legitimacy of this collaborative position.[8] As the dismal failure of the October 1, 1977 collaborative initiative clearly indicates, it may be very difficult to meet this domestic "policy legitimacy" constraint and convince Congress and the public of the desirability of the objectives which this posture seeks to promote. As Destler argues (in assessing the role of Congress in constraining American policy toward the Soviet Union),

agreements providing for limited *cooperation* [with Moscow] have proved to be vulnerable political targets because legislators use them as vehicles to pry new policy concessions from the Soviet government or from our own....Congress continues to be a volatile force on Soviet issues, usually pressing presidents toward a tougher line.[9]

Secondly, the parameters of the Soviet position regarding comprehensive settlement remained essentially unchanged during the period under consideration. Consequently, the Soviets "were hardly interested in peace at any price [and] would not pressure their clients more than the United States was visibly inclined to pressure Israel."[10] Hence any superpower agreement on the shaping of a regional settlement necessitates, as in October 1977, that American policy regarding the components of such an agreement be significantly modified.

Indeed, in order to meet this "Soviet constraint," Washington must formalize and legitimize the Soviet presence in the region — thus bolstering the USSR's status as a great power — and provide for a long-term Soviet role as a coguarantor or enforcer of peace. Such an agreement, observes Vital, "would have the added advantage [for Moscow] of implying, and perhaps even formalizing, an enduring division of the eastern Mediterranean into American and Russian spheres of influence."[11] And as Eran further indicates,

Moscow intends that any Arab-Israeli settlement be tied to the establishment of an international regime — one may call it Soviet-American condominium — which from time to time would require international policing; Moscow wishes to become co-gendarme of any Arab-Israeli settlement with the United States. The achievement of such a status in the region by the Soviet Union would mean, at long last, the formalization and legitimization of Soviet Middle Eastern involvement by the international community.[12]

Translated into concrete terms, an attempt by the US to join such a collaborative course entails the abandonment, explicitly or by implication, of certain positions to which it was hitherto clearly committed, e.g., its opposition to the establishment of an independent Palestinian state, or its refusal to involve the PLO in the peacemaking process prior to that organization's recognition of Israel's right to exist.

Here, then, is the paradox inherent in the collaborative strategy. The very nature of the modifications needed to meet the "Soviet

71

constraint" a priori guarantees the problematic nature of the task of mobilizing domestic and external support for the legitimacy of such a collaborative course. In this respect the costs, in terms of domestic support, of inducing Moscow into a collaborative design, are likely to be so high as to altogether deprive the administration of the necessary resources for implementing the strategy. The failure of Carter's October 1, 1977 initiative clearly demonstrates that the very effort to legitimize the Soviet role in the peacemaking process denied Washington the minimal base of domestic support without which implementation of this course was impossible.

True, in numerous public opinion surveys taken since 1978, a majority of respondents supported Soviet-American cooperation on such issues as energy and a nuclear freeze. However, this support was consistent with a concurrent strong public desire (at least until 1984, after which it abated considerably) "to increase defense spending and to adopt a tougher line [toward] the Soviet Union."[13] It therefore cannot be reconciled with a move held likely "to expand Soviet influence in the region."[14]

Similarly, since 1981 American public and congressional opinion has become increasingly ready to accept certain ad hoc coercive measures against Israel when the latter's conduct was perceived as exceeding those "legitimate security needs" which the public continued to support.[15] But these indications of erosion have yet to provide the administration with the necessary base of public support for a course which is likely to be widely interpreted as negatively affecting the very core of the "special relationship" between the United States and Israel.[16] Public and congressional criticism remains confined to relatively peripheral facets of Israel's behavior, and has not spilled over to such core issues as Israel's unwavering opposition to the establishment of an independent Palestinian state.[17] Essentially, then, any American attempt to change the rules of the game in the American-Israeli dyad by predicating a settlement on the premises of a de facto superpower condominium, is bound to encounter strong opposition in American public opinion, which still depicts Israel by and large as a fellow democracy and a viable bulwark against Soviet expansion.

In the words of Bernard Reich:

There is an element of cultural identity that sees Israel as a Western state in a sea of feudal, Oriental entities and as a perpetrator of the Judeo-Christian heritage...Israel is seen as having achieved substantial progress, despite its precarious existence, and as worthy of emulation. There is an historical affinity and similarity of national experience, which includes the immigrant and pioneering nature of the two states and their commitments to democracy. The US experience in striving to escape persecution and establish an independent national homeland has a parallel in a Jewish state in Palestine that appears to reaffirm these ideals through absorption and integration of immigrants in distress.[18]

During the period under scrutiny, these pervasive images of Israel "as a democratic nation and a society imbued with...libertarian values and humanistic culture" were reflected in a welter of public opinion surveys which, by and large, indicated considerable support for Israel. In general, sympathy for Israel has remained fairly constant over time, although there was an increase during and immediately after the 1967 and 1973 wars and in reaction to the completion of the Israeli withdrawal from Sinai in April 1982. Specifically, the findings of surveys taken between October 1973 and January 1985 show that whereas sympathy for the Arab states did not surpass 16 percent, support for Israel fluctuated between 44 percent and 56 percent. Similarly, during the same period, at least three out of four Americans polled held a positive image of Israel.[19] On the whole, examination of the prevailing attitudes of the American public, as well as of assorted leadership groups, to Middle Eastern issues during the period 1973-1985 suggests that, among those who have opinions on these matters, sympathy for Israel has always far outweighed support for the Arab cause, and cannot be explained solely as a residue of guilt feelings related to the Holocaust.

Within this context, the most effective guardian of those pro-Israel demarcation lines within which the US attempted to defuse the Arab-Israel predicament, has been the US Congress. The Congress' willingness to convert these somewhat amorphous sentiments into concrete pro-Israel legislation, has enabled it to assume over time a pivotal mediating role between mass public opinion and the executive branch. This has helped legitimize and sanction the activities of such interest groups as AIPAC. For many Americans, congressional backing for Israel has come to be expected almost axiomatically, irrespective of the ethnic or religious composition of a congressman's district.[20]

The Symington-Javits resolution of June 28, 1967, which had 63 sponsors; the Ribicoff-Scott statement of April 25, 1969, with 68 signatories; the Case-Tydings declaration of February 25, 1970, which had 70 signatories; Senator Scott's initiative of October 1, 1971, with its 78 sponsors; the letter sent to President Ford in May 1975 by 76 senators; and the congressional protest to President Carter (signed by 150 congressmen) in the wake of the October 1, 1977 communique — these are but a few illustrations of the widespread and durable nature of support for Israel in Congress.[21] In the words of William Quandt:

> Over the years, Congress has been much more responsive to pro-Israeli groups than to oil or Arab interests. About three-fourths of all senators, and a sizable majority of representatives, have put their names to pro-Israeli statements. The depth of commitment no doubt varies, as does the motivation, but when [the time comes] to vote on aid bills, for example, Israel can usually count on support.[22]

Clearly, any superpower initiative to translate into reality the vision of a regional condominium (or coimperium) cannot unfold in a political, social and psychological vacuum. In their effort to implement a "condominium strategy," American policymakers therefore have to cope with a welter of structural domestic constraints. In 1977, as we have seen, these actually compelled the US to forego its entire design.

Whether or not the makers of American Middle East diplomacy ultimately succeed in widening their *domestic* margin of maneuverability, they will still be confronted with "the external legitimacy constraint," namely, with the need to obtain adequate regional support for the legitimacy of their collaborative strategy.[23] However, as the case of the October 1, 1977 initiative again illustrates, the task of winning the support of the regional protagonists is likely to be no less arduous than the attempt to overcome domestic stumbling blocks on the road to a superpower settlement. In the first place, we have already noted that the implementation of a collaborative scenario bears directly on an entire complex of core values and interests pertaining to Israel's basic security needs. Hence, one can expect — as was the case in October 1977 — defiant Israeli behavior to persist even in the face of strong pressures.[24] For if it is convinced that compliance will endanger certain basic principles of its defense and foreign policy, Israel — feeling acutely threatened — is bound to demonstrate a higher level of resolve than its American ally, and will therefore be prepared to take greater risks and sacrifices.

To paraphrase George, a nation blessed with a superior will, whose commitment to certain values and courses of action (such as Israel's opposition to the creation of a Palestinian state, or to the involvement of the PLO in the peacemaking process) was established before the superpower initiative took place, is likely to fiercely resist the pressures exerted, and may ultimately prevail in the encounter despite its relative inferiority in terms of power capabilities.[25]

Israel's determination to defy its American ally in the wake of the October 1 initiative was not the only instance in which it effectively resisted Washington's peace plans in the Arab-Israeli sphere. In December 1969, the government of Golda Meir categorically rejected the Rogers Plan, and in March 1975, Jerusalem risked a confrontation with Ford and Kissinger when it insisted on a formal Egyptian statement proclaiming an end to the state of belligerency as a precondition for its withdrawal from the Mitla and Gidi passes. In embarking on a collision course with the US in 1975, Israel's policymakers could not, during most of the period under consideration, ignore global developments like the American abandonment of commitments to South Vietnam and the inability of the Ford administration to act firmly to resist Soviet and Soviet-proxy encroachment in third areas like Cambodia and Angola. These adverse developments considerably weakened the American signaling reputation and seriously eroded the image of resolve the US sought to project. Inevitably, during the period preceding the election of Ronald Reagan to the White House in 1980, they reduced the utility of total dependence on the US. America's small allies therefore became increasingly reluctant to lend their full and unmitigated support to a superpower which could not guarantee their security against external threats or subversion, and which was looked upon as lacking the necessary will to use power effectively.

In its resistance to a superpower collaborative design incorporating coercive elements, Israel is likely to be joined by other regional parties. Egypt, in particular, has on a number of occasions reiterated its opposition to various forms of superpower collaboration, and has reacted with defiance to what it perceived as an attempt to subordinate central tenets in its diplomacy to superpower considerations.[26] This may be illustrated by Cairo's reactions to several Soviet diplomatic moves which were perceived as reflecting the spirit of detente at the expense of Egypt's core interests and objectives on the Arab-Israeli front. Essentially, President Sadat may have viewed his actions of 1972-73 as at least partly generated by a Soviet orientation analogous to the multipolar-accommodative tendency.

At the time, Egypt was taking full advantage of the dynamics of a loose bipolar global system, and particularly of its own "reverse potentiality" (namely, its capacity to reverse the direction of its alliance with Moscow). Thus Cairo managed to acquire a degree of influence in its relations with the Soviet Union far out of proportion to its actual power.[27] It remained outside Moscow's recognized sphere of influence during most of Sadat's era, and despite huge Soviet investments in Egypt, the Soviet patron was unable to guarantee the loyal support of its Egyptian client. The latter, highly motivated to challenge the post-1967 territorial status quo, repeatedly sought to mobilize its limited capabilities in order to gain "influence parity" with Moscow. This was done by adopting recalcitrant retaliatory measures in the face of what was perceived in Cairo as a tacit understanding by both superpowers to manage the Arab-Israeli predicament in orderly, evolutionary, and incremental steps.[28]

For example, at the Moscow summit of May 1972 between Brezhnev and Nixon, Kissinger succeeded in inducing his Soviet hosts to agree to a very bland communique on the Middle East situation that was bound to be interpreted by President Sadat as a Soviet decision to put detente with the United States above any real assistance to the Arab cause against Israel.[29] As Kissinger acknowledges in his memoirs:

> The upshot [of the Soviet-American communique on the Middle East] was a meaningless paragraph that endorsed Security Council Resolution 242 and put the two sides on record as favoring peace in the Middle East. Calling as it did for 'peaceful settlement' and 'military relaxation' in the area, it was practically an implicit acceptance of the status quo and was bound to be taken ill not only in Cairo but elsewhere in the Arab world.[30]

Indeed, the joint statement of May 29, 1972 seemed to confirm Sadat's worst fears, convincing him that the superpowers had agreed to place the Middle East conflict on the back burner. As Alvin Rubinstein points out: "The Nixon-Brezhnev summit troubled Sadat. The low-key call for a political settlement; the lack of immediacy; the neglect of the Palestinians" — all contributed to Sadat's decision of July 1972 to expel Soviet military advisers from Egypt.[31] Mohamed Hassanein Heikal provides a vivid account of Sadat's mood upon learning of the outcome of the Nixon-Brezhnev meeting: "[Sadat] felt they [the Soviets] needed an electric shock. For four years first Nasser and then [Sadat] had been suffering at [Moscow's] hands. It was clear...that in Moscow the two super-powers had agreed that there was to be no war in the Middle East area."[32] On July 18 Sadat announced that "as of July 17, the Soviet military mission in Egypt had been terminated." Further, reiterating his opposition to "any [superpower] agreement to perpetuate the no-peace-no-war situation, [which] could in the long run beneficiate [sic] only Israel," the Egyptian president made clear his determination to proceed undeterred toward the accomplishment of such primary objectives as the disruption of the military and political status quo along the Suez canal: "We cannot abandon any of the [occupied] Arab lands....We make our own decisions and we take our positions in accordance with our own will. Our freedom is under our control."[33] Concurrent with the expulsion of approximately 20,000 Soviet military advisers, Sadat reactivated a secret channel of communications with the White House that he had initiated in April. From that time on, he pursued both the Soviet and American connections.

Moscow's muted reaction to the expulsion move clearly demonstrates how wide was Egypt's margin of maneuverability vis-à-vis its superpower patron. In this respect, the crisis in Egyptian-Soviet relations which was precipitated by the 1972 summit can be seen as but another milestone along a course which culminated — in the wake of the Yom Kippur War — in a major realignment between Cairo and Washington.

During the June 1973 San Clemente summit, a similar picture of convergence regarding at least some of the superpowers' regional interests and priorities emerged. The joint communique issued on June 25, 1973 asserted that the superpowers "would exert their efforts to promote the quickest possible settlement in the Middle East." Such a settlement, the document further stated, "should be in accordance with the interests of all states in the area, should be consistent with their independence and sovereignty, and should take into due account the legitimate interests of the Palestinian people."[34]

As was the case in the aftermath of the Moscow summit of May 1972, the June 1973 statement created the impression in Cairo that "both powers appeared to be content, at least for the time being, with the status quo and the preservation of the ceasefire." As Reich maintains, President Sadat was profoundly concerned "that the detente motives of the two superpowers would tend to assign a low priority to the Middle East." Convinced that the summit at least tacitly reaffirmed the status quo and thus reconfirmed the Israeli occupation of the Sinai Peninsula, Egypt reacted with defiance and accelerated its efforts to achieve "a greater degree of Arab unity and self reliance [which were] essential for the [forthcoming] battle against Israel. In this vein, the outcome of the June summit was — paradoxically — the reaffirmation of Sadat's decision to go to war."[35]

Indeed, in the wake of the 1973 summit, the Egyptian leadership became convinced that unless Egypt moved quickly to challenge the political and military balance of power, "detente will impose itelf on us before we can impose ourselves on it [and] will set conditions for the Middle East problem instead of the Middle East problem setting conditions for...detente." Sadat concluded that the Soviets would not help the Arabs recover their occupied territories, and set out to implement the next phase in his strategy — "a limited war in collaboration with Syria, designed to improve his bargaining position and create a crisis which the major powers could not ignore."[36]

As Sadat himself pointed out in a major foreign policy address delivered on July 23, 1973:

> We must make clear that we do not object to...detente per se, or to Soviet-American understanding, or to the elimination of the danger of total war from the world....At the same time, as we dwell in a sensitive region of the world, where both of these powers are present, we could not help asking about our interests, when both of these powers come to an agreed policy of their own....We must always consider the constraints governing Arab-Soviet cooperation, including international detente. We do not oppose world understanding and world peace, we simply want to solve our problem.[37]

After both summits, Egypt's perception of a sharply asymmetrical military situation proved the decisive factor within the Egyptian-Soviet dyad. Ultimately, with Cairo determined to challenge the post-1967 territorial status quo, Moscow had little choice but to acquiesce.

Lastly — and returning to the framework of American Middle East policy — Sadat was greatly incensed by the US-USSR October 1, 1977 declaration, as well as by the administration's inconsistency and vacillation in the face of the opposition to that initiative. Highly critical of the attempt to invite Moscow to reenter the diplomatic stage (and skeptical about Geneva as a forum for actual negotiations), Sadat sent his foreign minister Ismail Fahmi to Washington with a letter for President Carter, urging "that nothing be done to prevent Israel and Egypt from negotiating directly, with [the United States] serving as an intermediary before or after the Geneva conference is convened."[38] Frustrated and disenchanted with Carter's diplomacy, and faced with the prospect of an Arab veto of his negotiating strategy, Sadat embarked on his peace mission, thereby replacing the multilateral Geneva forum with bilateral channels of communication and negotiation.

Notwithstanding President Mubarak's slightly more accommodative posture toward the Soviet Union, he too is unlikely to acquiesce automatically in the face of a consolidated superpower position. Thus, in addition to the difficulties surrounding the attempt to meet the "domestic constraint," it is clear from these illustrations that the search for a joint superpower strategy in the Arab-Israeli sphere is bound to encounter strong opposition from some of the local parties, in particular during periods of a perceived asymmetrical military balance, even if we must assume that each local party would express its opposition quite separately. As Vital writes:

> neither of the two primary powers has significant influence on the internal dynamics of the regional conflict — if only because the disputants, Arabs and Jews, attach greater value to the achievement of the relations with that primary power on which they have tended to rely....On neither side is the relationship adequately summed up by the term "client" or "protege," as contemporary fashion would often have it.[39]

The more asymmetrical the perceived military and political balance between the local protagonists, and the wider the scope of those core interests whose preservation is perceived by one of the local disputants as threatened by the envisaged settlement, the less likely it is that the superpowers will successfully meet this external or regional constraint. The paradoxical corollary of this is that in order to be effective, a condominium strategy must obfuscate at least some of its wider dimensions and implications. Indeed, it is only when the insistence on comprehensiveness is traded for an almost unobtrusive, phased implementation, that a collaborative design has any prospects of even a modest measure of success.

Against this backdrop of multiple difficulties surrounding any attempt to consolidate both a domestic and an external base of support for promoting a superpower settlement, are we to conclude that the collaborative superpower strategy is doomed to failure? Certainly some of the regional preconditions for an effective pursuit of this posture have not materialized yet. One cannot, however, rule out the possibility that the domestic American environment will in the future become more receptive to the idea of a superpower settlement, thus providing American decisionmakers with an added margin of maneuverability. This scenario is supported by an analysis of the predominant trends in American public opinion between 1979 and 1984, which reveals a concurrent dual attitudinal pattern. On the one hand, the electorate has consistently expressed strong hostility toward the Soviet Union; on the other hand, it has advocated "no new foreign policy crusade" or highly dangerous involvement in crisis situations in such locales as El Salvador and the Middle East. Indeed, the period following the Soviet invasion of Afghanistan is clearly characterized by an ever growing complexity in both the structure and content of American public opinion, with the traditional dichotomies between simple left-right, hawk-dove orientations being progressively replaced by cluster of considerably more differentiated and subtle distinctions.[40] In the words of Yankelovich and Doble:

> The public is now [in 1984] having second thoughts about the dangers of...an assertive posture [vis-à-vis the Soviet Union] at a time when the United States is no longer seen to maintain nuclear supremacy. The electorate is still wary, still mistrustful, and still convinced that the Soviets will seize every possible advantage they can; yet, at the same time, Americans are determined to stop what they see as a drift toward...[superpower] confrontation....The stage is being set for a new phase in our relationship with the Soviets.[41]

Indeed, while still supporting a firm containment posture vis-à-vis the Soviet Union, most Americans consistently indicated

— during the course of Reagan's first term in office — a strong preference for keeping the United States out of local conflicts. Similarly, while the desire to deter and contain Soviet encroachment has remained strong in American public opinion since the invasion of Afghanistan, this bipolar-confrontational trend has been subordinated on numerous occasions to what has been perceived by the public as the more compelling need to minimize the risks of superpower conflagration by concluding a series of agreements on arms control issues.

As Schneider points out, an atmosphere of strong anti-Soviet feeling has given rise to public fear and insecurity and, consequently, to a demand for arms control. At the end of 1982, 58 percent of the public said they favored "a mutual, verifiable freeze on nuclear weapons...right now, if the Soviets would agree." Only 21 percent endorsed President Reagan's position that such a freeze should be agreed to "only after the US builds up its nuclear weapons more," while 12 percent opposed a freeze altogether. Thus while the public appeared "to approve of Reagan's initial defense buildup and his tough anti-Soviet line," it was apprehensive of the "greater risk of war" inherent in this policy. People therefore demanded "some assurances that the president was equally strong in his commitment to peace and arms control."[42]

Here, then, is evidence of a growing American domestic willingness to endorse a collaborative superpower strategy on those occasions where the dangers of escalation and confrontation are perceived as acute. Against such a backdrop, erosion of long-standing public opposition to a collaborative strategy in the Middle East cannot be ruled out. Combined with a consistent Soviet desire to avoid *direct* regional confrontations with the United States and thus to control the risks of escalation inherent in such areas as the Middle East, this convergence of Soviet and American predilections may potentially precipitate a superpower understanding on at least some of the parameters of peace.

Needless to say, such a development will not come about overnight. The failure of the Geneva superpower summit of November 1985 to reach any understanding on the parameters of a Middle East settlement clearly underscores this fact. Nor do we envisage the complete abandonment of America's "special relationship" with Israel. Nevertheless, it is possible that in the wake of a period of incessant, potentially explosive crises of the sort precipitated by the June 1982 Lebanon War, the American public will increasingly support a joint superpower action designed to stabilize, at long last, an endemically tense situation. Such an agreement — in the aftermath of which at least a partial American disengagement from the region would become possible — is likely to be particularly popular with that "large, inattentive public" whose foreign policy orientation is labeled by Schneider as "noninternationalist."[43] Although unorganized and somewhat amorphous, this group is "predisposed against American involvement in other countries' affairs unless a clear and compelling issue of national interest or national security is at stake....Noninternationalists...see no point to American involvement in most of the world. They are against foreign aid, against troop involvement, against anything that smacks of foreign entanglement."[44]

These noninternationalist trends are reinforced by the emergence of more articulate, elitist neoisolationist sentiments on the American political scene, as reflected in the desire to limit security commitments to the "indispensable minimum."[45] Potentially they provide future administrations with the necessary public infrastructure for the effective pursuit of a posture of "disengagement by agreement."[46] Yet even were such a scenario to take place, it is by no means certain that Washington's decisionmakers would manage to secure the acquiescence, let alone the support of the local parties, whose strong disinclination to accommodate themselves to such a strategy proved so effective in thwarting the October 1, 1977 initiative.

In conclusion, one cannot rule out the possibility that a superpower understanding on the parameters of regional peace will ultimately emerge. Nevertheless, it is reasonable to expect that, at least in the foreseeable future, the US and the USSR will continue to rely largely on partial, tacit understandings and informal patterns of restraint in approaching the Arab-Israeli predicament.[47] Such norms are invariably precarious and uncertain in anything but the short run.[48] Hence it is virtually certain that, from a superpower standpoint, the Middle East will continue to be permeated with tension and animosity. Unless, of course, the local protagonists themselves at long last succeed in defusing the protracted conflict.[49]

Appendices

I. The Pure Bipolar-Confrontational Conception: Presentation

Address by President Reagan to Members of British Parliament, June 8, 1982. Weekly Compilation of Presidential Documents 18 (1982), pp. 764-768.

Well, from here I will go to Bonn and then Berlin, where there stands a grim symbol of power untamed. The Berlin Wall, that dreadful gray gash across the city, is in its third decade. It is the fitting signature of the regime that built it....

We're approaching the end of a bloody century plagued by a terrible political invention — totalitarianism. Optimism comes less easily today, not because democracy is less vigorous, but because democracy's enemies have refined their instruments of repression. Yet optimism is in order, because day by day democracy is proving itself to be a not-at-all-fragile flower. From Stettin on the Baltic to Varna on the Black Sea, the regimes planted by totalitarianism have had more than 30 years to establish their legitimacy. But none — not one regime — has yet been able to risk free elections. Regimes planted by bayonets do not take root....

Now, I am aware that among us here and throughout Europe there is legitimate disagreement over the extent to which the public sector should play a role in a nation's economy and life. But on one point all of us are united — our abhorrence of dictatorship in all its forms, but most particularly totalitarianism and the terrible inhumanities it has caused in our time — the great purge, Auschwitz and Dachau, the Gulag, and Cambodia.

Historians looking back at our time will note the consistent restraint and peaceful intentions of the West. They will note that it was the democracies who refused to use the threat of their nuclear monopoly in the forties and early fifties for territorial or imperial gain. Had that nuclear monopoly been in the hands of the Communist world, the map of Europe — indeed, the world — would look very different today. And certainly they will note it was not the democracies that invaded Afghanistan or suppressed Polish Solidarity or used chemical and toxin warfare in Afghanistan and Southeast Asia.

If history teaches anything it teaches that self-delusion in the face of unpleasant facts is folly. We see around us today the marks of our terrible dilemma — predictions of doomsday, antinuclear demonstrations, an arms race in which the West must, for its own protection, be an unwilling participant. At the same time we see totalitarian forces in the world who seek subversion and conflict around the globe to further their barbarous assault on the human spirit. What, then, is our course? Must civilization perish in a hail of fiery atoms? Must freedom wither in a quiet, deadening accommodation with totalitarian evil?

Sir Winston Churchill refused to accept the inevitability of war or even that it was imminent. He said, "I do not believe that Soviet Russia desires war. What they desire is the fruits of war and the indefinite expansion of their power and doctrines. But what we have to consider here today while time remains is the permanent prevention of war and the establishment of conditions of freedom and democracy as rapidly as possible in all countries."

Well, this is precisely our mission today: to preserve freedom as well as peace. It may not be easy to see, but I believe we live now at a turning point.

In an ironic sense Karl Marx was right. We are witnessing today a great revolutionary crisis, a crisis where the demands of the economic order are conflicting directly with those of the political order. But the crisis is happening not in the free, non-Marxist West, but in the home of Marxist-Leninism, the Soviet Union. It is the Soviet Union that runs against the tide of history by denying human freedom and human dignity to its citizens. It also is in deep economic difficulty. The rate of growth in the national product has been steadily declining since the fifties and is less than half of what it was then.

The dimensions of this failure are astounding. A country which employs one-fifth of its population in agriculture is unable to feed its own people. Were it not for the private sector, the tiny private sector tolerated in Soviet agriculture, the country might be on the brink of famine. These private plots occupy a bare 3 percent of the arable land but account for nearly one-quarter of Soviet farm output and nearly one-third of meat products and vegetables. Overcentralized, with little or no incentives, year after year the Soviet system pours its best resource into the making of instruments of destruction. The constant shrinkage of economic growth combined with the growth of military production is putting a heavy strain on the Soviet people. What we see here is a political structure that no longer corresponds to its economic base, a society where productive forces are hampered by political ones.

The decay of the Soviet experiment should come as no surprise to us. Wherever the comparisons have been made between free and closed societies — West Germany and East Germany, Austria and Czechoslovakia, Malaysia and Vietnam — it is the democratic countries that are prosperous and responsive to the needs of their people. And one of the simple but overwhelming facts of our time is this: Of all the millions of refugees we've seen in the modern world, their flight is always away from, not toward the Communist world. Today on the NATO line, our military forces face east to prevent a possible invasion. On the other side of the line, the Soviet forces also face east to prevent their people from leaving.

The hard evidence of totalitarian rule has caused in mankind an uprising of the intellect and will. Whether it is the growth of the new schools of economics in America or England or the appearance of the so-called new philosophers in France, there is one unifying thread running through the intellectual work of these groups — rejection of the arbitrary power of the state, the refusal to subordinate the rights of the individual to the superstate, the realization that collectivism stifles all the best human impulses....

In the Communist world, man's instinctive desire for freedom and self-determination surfaces again and again. To be sure, there are grim reminders of how brutally the police state attempts to snuff out this quest for self-rule — 1953 in East Germany, 1956 in Hungary, 1968 in Czechoslovakia, 1981 in Poland. But the struggle continues in Poland. And we know that there are even those who strive and suffer from freedom within the confines of the Soviet Union itself. How we conduct ourselves here in the Western democracies will determine whether this trend continues.

No, democracy is not a fragile flower. Still it needs cultivating. If the rest of this country is to witness the gradual growth of freedom and democratic ideals, we must take actions to assist the campaign for democracy.

Some argue that we should encourage democratic change in right-wing dictatorships, but not in Communist regimes. Well, to accept this preposterous notion — as some well-meaning people have — is to invite the argument that once countries achieve a nuclear capability, they should be allowed an undisturbed reign of terror over their own citizens. We reject this course.

As for the Soviet view, Chairman Brezhnev repeatedly has

stressed that the competition of ideas and systems must continue and that this is entirely consistent with relaxation of tensions and peace.

Well, we ask only that these systems begin by living up to their own constitutions, abiding by their own laws, and complying with the international obligations they have undertaken. We ask only for a process, a direction, a basic code of decency, not for an instant transformation.

We cannot ignore the fact that even without our encouragement there has been and will continue to be repeated explosions against repression and dictatorships. The Soviet Union itself is not immune to this reality. Any system is inherently unstable that has no peaceful means to legitimize its leaders. In such cases, the very repressiveness of the state ultimately drives people to resist it, if necessary, by force.

While we must be cautious about forcing the pace of change, we must not hesitate to declare our ultimate objectives and to take concrete actions to move toward them. We must be staunch in our conviction that freedom is not the sole prerogative of a lucky few, but the inalienable and universal right of all human beings. So states the United Nations Universal Declaration of Human Rights, which, among other things, guarantees free elections.

The objective I propose is quite simple to state: to foster the infrastructure of democracy, the system of a free press, unions, political parties, universities, which allows a people to choose their own way to develop their own culture, to reconcile their own differences through peaceful means....

We in America now intend to take additional steps, as many of our allies have already done, toward realizing this same goal....

It is time that we committed ourselves as a nation — in both the public and private sectors — to assisting democratic development.

II. Reagan and the Pure Bipolar-Confrontational Conception: Application and Transformation

Address by President Reagan before the 39th Session of the General Assembly in New York on September 24, 1984.*Bulletin* **LXXXIV (November 1984): pp. 3-7.**

For 35 years, the North Atlantic alliance has guaranteed the peace in Europe. In both Europe and Asia, our alliances have been the vehicle for a great reconciliation among nations that had fought bitter wars in decades and centuries past. And here in the Western Hemisphere, north and south are being lifted on the tide of freedom and are joined in a common effort to foster peaceful economic development.

We're proud of our association with all those countries that share our commitment to freedom, human rights, the rule of law — and international peace. Indeed, the bulwark of security that the democratic alliance provides is essential — and remains essential — to the maintenance of world peace. Every alliance involves burdens and obligations, but these are far less than the risks and sacrifices that would result if the peace-loving nations were divided and neglectful of their common security. The people of the United States will remain faithful to their commitments....

The United States welcomes diversity and peaceful competition; we do not fear the trends of history. We are not ideologically rigid; we do have principles and we will stand by them, but we will also seek the friendship and goodwill of all, both old friends and new....

The Middle East has known more than its share of tragedy and conflict for decades, and the United States has been actively involved in peace diplomacy for just as long. We consider ourselves a full partner in the quest for peace. The record of the 11 years since the October war shows that much can be achieved through negotiations. It also shows that the road is long and hard.

Two years ago, I proposed a fresh start toward a negotiated solution to the Arab-Israeli conflict. My initiative of September 1, 1982, contains a set of positions that can serve as a basis for a just and lasting peace. That initiative remains a realistic and workable approach, and I am committed to it as firmly as on the day I announced it. And the foundation stone of this effort remains Security Council Resolution 242, which in turn was incorporated in all its parts in the Camp David accords....

The lesson of experience is that negotiation works. The peace treaty between Israel and Egypt brought about the peaceful return of the Sinai, clearly showing that the negotiating process brings results when the parties commit themselves to it. The time is bound to come when the same wisdom and courage will be applied, with success, to reach peace between Israel and all of its Arab neighbors in a manner that assures security for all in the region, the recognition of Israel, and a solution to the Palestinian problem.

In every part of the world, the United States is similarly engaged in peace diplomacy as an active player or a strong supporter....

The United States has been, and always will be, a friend of peaceful solutions.

This is not less true with respect to my country's relations with the Soviet Union. When I appeared before you last year, I noted that we cannot count on the instinct for survival alone to protect us against war. Deterrence is necessary but not sufficient. America has repaired its strength; we have invigorated our alliances and friendships. We're ready for constructive negotiations with the Soviet Union.

We recognize that there is no sane alternative to negotiations on arms control and other issues between our two nations, which have the capacity to destroy civilization as we know it. I believe this is a view shared by virtually every country in the world, and by the Soviet Union itself.

And I want to speak to you today on what the United States and the Soviet Union can accomplish together in the coming years and the concrete steps we need to take.

You know, as I stand here and look out from this podium — there in front of me — I can see the seat of the representative from the Soviet Union. And not far from that seat, just over to the side, is the seat of the representative from the United States.

In this historic assembly hall, it's clear there is not a great distance between us. Outside this room, while there will still be clear differences, there is every reason why we should do all that is possible to shorten that distance. And that's why we're here. Isn't that what this organization is all about?

Last January 16, I set out three objectives for US-Soviet relations that can provide an agenda for our work over the months ahead. First, I said, we need to find ways to reduce — and eventually to eliminate — the threat and use of force in solving international disputes. Our concern over the potential for nuclear war cannot deflect us from the terrible human tragedies occurring every day in the regional conflicts I just discussed. Together, we have a particular responsibility to contribute to political solutions to these problems, rather than to exacerbate them through the provision of even more weapons.

I propose that our two countries agree to embark on periodic consultations at policy level about regional problems. We will be prepared, if the Soviets agree, to make senior experts available at regular intervals for in-depth exchanges of views. I have asked Secretary Shultz to explore this with Foreign Minister Gromyko. Spheres of influence are a thing of the past. Differences between American and Soviet interests are not. The objectives of this political dialogue will be to help avoid miscalculation, reduce the potential risk of US-Soviet confrontation, and help the people in areas of conflict to find peaceful solutions.

The United States and the Soviet Union have achieved agreements of historic importance on some regional issues. The Austrian State Treaty and the Berlin accords are notable and lasting examples. Let us resolve to achieve similar agreements...

Our second task must be to find ways to reduce the vast stockpiles of armaments in the world. I am committed to redoubling our negotiating efforts to achieve real results: in Geneva, a complete ban on chemical weapons; in Vienna, real reductions — to lower and equal levels — in Soviet and American, Warsaw Pact and NATO, conventional forces; in Stockholm, concrete practical measures to enhance mutual confidence, to reduce the risk of war, and to reaffirm commitments concerning non-use of force; in the field of nuclear testing, improvements in verification essential to ensure compliance with the Threshold Test Ban and Peaceful Nuclear Explosions agreements; and in the field of nonproliferation, close cooperation to strengthen the international institutions and practices aimed at halting the spread of nuclear weapons, together with redoubled efforts to meet the legitimate expectations of all nations that the Soviet Union and the United States will substantially reduce their own nuclear arsenals. We and the Soviets have agreed to upgrade our "hot line" communications facility, and our discussions of nuclear nonproliferation in recent years have been useful to both sides. We think there are other possibilities for improving communications in this area that deserve serious exploration.

I believe the proposal of the Soviet Union for opening US-Soviet talks in Vienna provided an important opportunity to advance these objectives. We've been prepared to discuss a wide range of issues and concerns of both sides, such as the relationship between defensive and offensive forces and what has been called the militarization of space. During the talks, we would consider what measures of restraint both sides might take while negotiations proceed. However, any agreement must logically depend upon our ability to get the competition in offensive arms under control and to achieve genuine stability at substantially lower levels of nuclear arms.

Our approach in all these areas will be designed to take into account concerns the Soviet Union has voiced. It will attempt to provide a basis for a historic breakthrough in arms control. I'm disappointed that we were not able to open our meeting in Vienna earlier this month, on the date originally proposed by the Soviet Union. I hope we can begin these talks by the end of the year or shortly thereafter.

The third task I set in January was to establish a better working relationship between the Soviet Union and the United States, one marked by greater cooperation and understanding.

We've made some modest progress. We have reached agreements to improve our "hot line," extend our 10-year economic agreement, enhance consular cooperation, and explore coordination of search and rescue efforts at sea.

We've also offered to increase significantly the amount of US grain for purchase by the Soviets and to provide the Soviets a direct fishing allocation off US coasts. But there is much more we could do together. I feel particularly strongly about breaking down the barriers between the peoples of the United States and the Soviet Union and among our political, military, and other leaders. All of these steps that I have mentioned, and especially the arms control negotiations, are extremely important to a step-by-step process toward peace. But let me also say that we need to extend the arms control process, to build a bigger umbrella under which it can operate — a roadmap, if you will, showing where, during the next 20 years or so, these individual efforts can lead.

This can greatly assist step-by-step negotiations and enable us to avoid having all our hopes or expectations ride on any single set or series of negotiations. If progress is temporarily halted at one set of talks, this newly established framework for arms control could help us take up the slack at other negotiations.

Today, to the great end of lifting the dread of nuclear war from the peoples of the earth, I invite the leaders of the world to join in a new beginning. We need a fresh approach to reducing international tensions. History demonstrates beyond controversy that, just as the arms competition has its roots in political suspicions and anxieties, so it can be channeled in more stabilizing directions and eventually be eliminated, if those political suspicions and anxieties are addressed as well. Toward this end, I will suggest to the Soviet Union that we institutionalize regular ministerial or cabinet-level meetings between our two countries on the whole agenda of issues before us, including the problem of needless obstacles to understanding. To take but one idea for discussion: in such talks we could consider the exchange of outlines of 5-year military plans for weapons development and our schedules of intended procurement. We would also welcome the exchange of observers at military exercises and locations. And I propose that we find a way for Soviet experts to come to the US nuclear test site, and for ours to go to theirs, to measure directly the yields of tests of nuclear weapons. We should work toward having such arrangements in place by next spring.

I hope that the Soviet Union will cooperate in this undertaking and reciprocate in a manner that will enable the two countries to establish the base for verification for effective limits on underground nuclear testing....

III. The Mitigated Bipolar-Confrontational Conception: Presentation

Detente with the Soviet Union: The Reality of Competition and the Imperative of Cooperation

Statement of Secretary Kissinger, presented to the Senate Committee on Foreign Relations, September 19, 1974. *Bulletin* **LXXI (July 1-December 30, 1974), pp. 505-518.**

Since the dawn of the nuclear age, the world's fears of holocaust and its hopes for peace have turned on the relationship between the United States and the Soviet Union.

Throughout history men have sought peace but suffered war; all too often, deliberate decisions or miscalculations have brought violence and destruction to a world yearning for tranquility. Tragic as the consequences of violence may have been in the past, the issue of peace and war takes on unprecedented urgency when, for the first time in history, two nations have the capacity to destroy mankind. In the nuclear age, as President Eisenhower pointed out two decades ago, "there is no longer any alternative to peace."

The destructiveness of modern weapons defines the necessity of the task; deep differences in philosophy and interests between the United States and the Soviet Union point up its difficulty. These differences do not spring from misunderstanding or personalities or transitory factors:

— They are rooted in history and in the way the two countries have developed.

— They are nourished by conflicting values and opposing ideologies.

— They are expressed in diverging national interests that produce political and military competition.

— They are influenced by allies and friends whose association we value and whose interests we will not sacrifice.

Paradox confuses our perception of the problem of peaceful coexistence: if peace is pursued to the exclusion of any other goal, other values will be compromised and perhaps lost; but if unconstrained rivalry leads to nuclear conflict, these values, along with everything else, will be destroyed in the resulting holocaust. However competitive they may be at some levels of their relationship, both major nuclear powers must base their policies on the premise that neither can expect to impose its will on the other without running an intolerable risk. The challenge of our time is to reconcile the reality of competition with the imperative of coexistence.

There can be no peaceful international order without a constructive relationship between the United States and the Soviet Union. There will be no international stability unless both the Soviet Union and the United States conduct themselves with restraint and unless they use their enormous power for the benefit of mankind.

Thus we must be clear at the outset on what the term "detente" entails. It is the search for a more constructive relationship with the Soviet Union reflecting the realities I have outlined. It is a continuing process, not a final condition that has been or can be realized at any one specific point in time. And it has been pursued by successive American leaders, though the means have varied as have world conditions.

Some fundamental principles guide this policy:

The United States cannot base its policy solely on Moscow's good intentions. But neither can we insist that all forward movement must await a convergence of American and Soviet purposes. We seek, regardless of Soviet intentions, to serve peace through a systematic resistance to pressure and conciliatory responses to moderate behavior.

We must oppose aggressive actions and irresponsible behavior. But we must not seek confrontation lightly.

We must maintain a strong national defense while recognizing that in the nuclear age the relationship between military strength and politically usable power is the most complex in all history.

Where the age-old antagonism between freedom and tyranny is concerned, we are not neutral. But other imperatives impose limits on our ability to produce internal changes in foreign countries. Consciousness of our limits is recognition of the necessity of peace — not moral callousness. The preservation of human life and human society are moral values, too.

We must be mature enough to recognize that to be stable a relationship must provide advantages to both sides and that the most constructive international relationships are those in which both parties perceive an element of gain. Moscow will benefit from certain measures, just as we will from others. The balance cannot be struck on each issue every day, but only over the whole range of relations and over a period of time....

Most Americans perceive relations between states as either friendly or hostile, both defined in nearly absolute terms. Soviet foreign policy, by comparison, is conducted in a grey area heavily influenced by the Soviet conception of the balance of forces. Thus Soviet diplomacy is never free of tactical pressures or adjustments, and it is never determined in isolation from the prevailing military balance. For Moscow, East-West contacts and negotiations are in part designed to promote Soviet influence abroad, especially in Western Europe — and to gain formal acceptance of those elements of the status quo most agreeable to Moscow.

The issue, however, is not whether peace and stability serve Soviet purposes, but whether they serve our own. Indeed, to the extent that our attention focuses largely on Soviet intentions we create a latent vulnerability. If detente can be justified only by a basic change in Soviet motivation, the temptation becomes overwhelming to base US-Soviet relations not on realistic appraisal but on tenuous hopes: a change in Soviet tone is taken as a basic change of philosophy. Atmosphere is confused with substance. Policy oscillates between poles of suspicion and euphoria.

Neither extreme is realistic, and both are dangerous. The hopeful view ignores that we and the Soviet are bound to compete for the foreseeable future. The pessimistic view ignores that we have some parallel interests and that we are compelled to coexist. Detente encourages an environment in which competitors can regulate and restrain their differences and ultimately move from competition to cooperation....

In the postwar period repeated efforts were made to improve our relationship with Moscow. The spirits of Geneva, Camp David, and Glassboro were evanescent moments in a quarter century otherwise marked by tensions and by sporadic confrontation. What is new in the current period of relaxation of tensions is its duration, the scope of the relationship which has evolved, and the continuity and intensity of consultation which it has produced.

For the United States the choice was clear: to provide as many incentives as possible for those actions by the Soviet Union most conducive to peace and individual well-being and to overcome the swings between illusionary optimism and harsh antagonism that had characterized most of the postwar period.... We sought to explore every avenue toward an honorable and just accommodation while remaining determined not to settle for mere atmospherics. We relied on a balance of mutual interests rather than Soviet intentions. When challenged — such as in the Middle East, the Caribbean, or Berlin — we always responded firmly. And when Soviet policy moved toward conciliation, we sought to turn what may have started as a tactical maneuver into a durable pattern of conduct.

Our approach proceeds from the conviction that, in moving forward across a wide spectrum of negotiations, progress in one area adds momentum to progress in other areas. If we succeed, then no agreement stands alone as an isolated accomplishment vulnerable to the next crisis. We did not invent the interrelationship between issues expressed in the so-called linkage concept; it was a reality because of the range of problems and areas in which the interests of the United States and the Soviet Union impinge on each other. We have looked for progress in a series of agreements settling specific political issues, and we have sought to relate these to a new standard of international conduct appropriate to the dangers of the nuclear age. By acquiring a stake in this network of relationships with the West, the Soviet Union may become more conscious of what it would lose by a return to confrontation. Indeed, it is our hope that it will develop a self-interest in fostering the entire process of relaxation of tensions.... It was difficult in the past to speak of a US-Soviet bilateral relationship in any normal sense of the phrase. Trade was negligible. Contacts between various institutions and between the peoples of the two countries were at best sporadic. There were no cooperative efforts in science and technology. Cultural exchange was modest. As a result, there was no tangible inducement toward cooperation and no penalty for aggressive behavior. Today, by joining our efforts even in such seemingly apolitical fields as medical research or environmental protection, we and the Soviets can benefit not only our two peoples but all mankind; in addition, we generate incentives for restraint....

To be sure, the process of detente raises serious issues for many people. Let me deal with these in terms of the principles which underline our policy.

First, if detente is to endure, both sides must benefit.

There is no question that the Soviet Union obtains benefits from detente. On what other grounds would the tough-minded members of the Politburo sustain it? But the essential point surely must be that detente serves American and world interests as well. If these coincide with some Soviet interests, this will only strengthen the durability of the process.

On the global scale, in terms of the conventional measures of power, influence, and position, our interests have not suffered — they have generally prospered. In many areas of the world, the influence and the respect we enjoy are greater than was the case for many years. It is also true that Soviet influence and presence are felt in many parts of the world. But this is a reality that would exist without detente. The record shows that detente does not deny us the opportunity to react to it and to offset it.

Our bilateral relations with the USSR are beginning to proliferate across a broad range of activities in our societies. Many of the projects now underway are in their infancy; we have many safeguards against unequal benefits — in our laws, in the agreements themselves, and in plain common sense. Of course, there are instances where the Soviet Union has obtained some particular advantage. But we seek in each agreement or project to provide for benefits that are mutual. We attempt to make sure that there are trade-offs among the various programs that are implemented. Americans surely are the last who need fear hard bargaining or lack confidence in competition.

Second, building a new relationship with the Soviet Union does not entail any devaluation of traditional alliance relations.

Our approach to relations with the USSR has always been, and will continue to be, rooted in the belief that the cohesion of our alliances, and particularly the Atlantic alliance, is a precondition to establishing a more constructive relationship with the USSR.

Crucial, indeed unique, as may be our concern with Soviet power, we do not delude ourselves that we should deal with it alone. When we speak of Europe and Japan as representing centers of power and influence, we describe not merely an observable fact but an indispensable element in the equilibrium needed to keep the world at peace. The cooperation and partnership between us transcend formal agreements; they reflect values and traditions not soon, if ever, to be shared with our adversaries....

Third, the emergence of more normal relations with the Soviet Union must not undermine our resolve to maintain our national defense.

There is a tendency in democratic societies to relax as dangers seem to recede; there is an inclination to view the maintenance of strength as incompatible with relaxation of tensions rather than its precondition. But this is primarily a question of leadership. We shall attempt to be vigilant to the dangers facing America. This administration will not be misled — or mislead — on issues of national defense. At the same time, we do not accept the proposition that we need crises to sustain our defense. A society that needs artificial crises to do what is needed for survival will soon find itself in mortal danger.

Fourth, we must know what can and cannot be achieved in changing human conditions in the East.

The question of dealing with Communist governments has troubled the American people and the Congress since 1917. There has always been a fear that by working with a government whose internal policies differ so sharply with our own we are in some manner condoning these policies or encouraging their continuation. Some argue that until there is a genuine "liberalization" — or signs of serious progress in this direction — all elements of conciliation in Soviet policy must be regarded as temporary and tactical. In that view, demands for internal changes must be the precondition for the pursuit of a relaxation of tensions with the Soviet Union.

Our view is different. We shall insist on responsible international behavior by the Soviet Union and use it as the primary index of our relationship. Beyond this we will use our influence to the maximum to alleviate suffering and to respond to humane appeals. We know what we stand for, and we shall leave no doubt about it.

IV. Kissinger's Exclusionist Diplomacy, 1973-75 and the Mitigated Bipolar-Confrontational Conception: Application

Global Peace, The Middle East, and the United States

Address by Secretary Kissinger, at Cincinnati, Ohio before the Greater Cincinnati Chamber of Commerce, September 16, 1975. *Bulletin* LXXIII (October 6, 1975), pp. 496-500.

...The Middle East lies at the crossroads of three continents. Because of the area's strategic importance and because it provides the energy on which much of the world depends, outside powers have continued to involve themselves in its conflicts, often competitively.

For the United States a diplomatic role in the Middle East is not a preference, but a matter of vital interest:

— Because of our historical and moral commitment to the survival and security of Israel;

— Because of our important concerns in the Arab world, an area of more than 150 million people and the site of the world's largest oil reserves;

— Because perpetual crisis in the Middle East would severely strain our relations with our most important allies in Europe and Japan;

— Because upheaval in the Middle East jeopardizes the world's hopes for economic recovery, threatening the well-being of the industrial nations and the hopes of the developing world; and

— Because tension in the Middle East increases the prospect of direct US-Soviet confrontation with its attendant nuclear risk.

Each successive Middle East crisis has presented us with painful choices between our many commitments and interests. And each successive crisis accelerates the trends of radicalism in the area, putting greater pressures on America's friends in the moderate Arab world, and heightening all the tensions and dangers....We have no illusions about the difficulties. The Middle East has seen more than its share of dashed hopes and disappointment. But progress depends crucially — even decisively — on the United States. Time and again the parties have turned to us for mediation. Time and again we have acceded to these requests because we are convinced that stagnation invites disaster. The next Middle East war will pose greater risks, complexities, and dangers and cause more dislocations than any previous conflict.

What, then, has been our approach?

For nearly three decades it was axiomatic that *all* issues pertaining to *all* the countries involved had to be addressed comprehensively: the final frontiers of Israel and the reciprocal guarantees of peace of the Arab states, the future of the Palestinians, the status of Jerusalem, and the question of international guarantees should all be considered together.

But for 30 years it proved nearly impossible even to begin the process of negotiation. Every attempt to discuss a comprehensive solution failed — from the partition plan, to the Lausanne conference [1949], to the Rogers plan and the Four-Power talks of 1969 and 1970, to the UN Security Council deliberations. To discuss simultaneously issues of such complexity, between countries whose deep mutual mistrust rejected even the concept of compromise, was futile until a minimum of confidence had been established. In the long history of the Arab-Israeli conflict, it is a new and relatively recent development that opinion in the Arab world has begun to think in terms of recognizing a sovereign Israel and that Israel has begun to see peace as a tangible goal rather than a distant dream.

The United States therefore concluded that instead of seeking to deal with all problems at once, we should proceed step by step with the parties prepared to negotiate and on the issues where some room for maneuver seemed possible. We believed that once the parties began a negotiating process they would develop a stake in success. Solutions to problems more easily negotiable would build mutual confidence. On each side a sense would grow that negotiations could produce benefits and that agreements would be kept — agreements that could become building blocks for a final peace.

Ultimately we expected that the step-by-step process would bring about, for the first time, the basic political conditions needed for the overall settlement called for by Security Council Resolution 338. This remains our goal....

The Egyptian-Israeli agreement is a step in a continuing process. The agreement states explicitly that the parties shall continue the negotiating efforts to reach an overall final peace settlement in accordance with Resolution 338....For our part, we stand ready to assist as the parties desire. We will seriously encourage a negotiation between Syria and Israel. We are prepared to consult all countries concerned, including the Soviet Union, about the timing and substance of a reconvened Geneva Conference. And we are fully aware that there will be no permanent peace unless it includes arrangements that take into account the legitimate interests of the Palestinian people.

The United States seeks no special advantage in the Middle East. It has always been our policy that the nations of the region should be free to determine their own relationships with any outside power. Therefore the United States would not understand, and would be obliged to oppose, efforts by any outside power to thwart the Egyptian-Israeli agreement.

In the search for a final peace, the United States is prepared to work with the Soviet Union. We are cosponsors of the Security Council resolutions that launched this hopeful course of negotiation; we are cochairmen of the Geneva Peace Conference, which met at an early crucial phase. While we have had important differences with the Soviet Union over the substance of a settlement, our two countries have held parallel views that the Middle East situation poses grave dangers and that partial steps must be part of, and contribute to, progress toward a comprehensive solution.

In the Middle East there is a yearning for peace surpassing any known for a generation. Let us seize this historic opportunity. The suffering and bravery of the people of the Middle East demand it; the highest interests of the United States require it.

This is why the American people, their Congress, and the President are, to an extraordinary degree, united on the course of our Middle East policy. And this is why we will not cease our effort.

V. Kissinger's Exclusionist Diplomacy, 1973-75, and the Mitigated Bipolar-Confrontational Conception: Reassessment

Secretary Kissinger Interviewed at Annual Meeting of the American Society of Newspaper Editors in Washington on April 13, 1976, *Bulletin* LXXIV (May 3, 1976), pp. 570-571

Q: Mr. (Edwin M.) Yoder *(The Washington Star):*

Mr. Secretary, it seems to me the most striking thing about the things said by your distinguished opposition critics this morning, or the most striking premise, was that the United States was still in a situation in which it can define problems in the world and then present its definition for discussion as an agenda. And to this end, on the question of the Middle East, it was said that generally your diplomacy, your step-by-step diplomacy in the Middle East, had taken the problem at the wrong end. What should be done, as I understood the proposition, was that the United States should put forward a plan taking into account the very long-distance, long-run objectives for a stable peace in that area and then say to the potential belligerents — active or potential belligerents in that case — "Here it is, let's have your remarks on this solution of the problem." Could you comment on that?

Secretary Kissinger:

Yes. First of all, the differences between your views and those of our critics very significantly concerns the question of timing. We have always recognized that at some point in the peacemaking process there would have to be a comprehensive approach rather than a step-by-step approach.

The difference between my views and those of my distinguished presumptive successors [laughter] is their retrospective view that we should have done this in 1973. Now, it can, of course, never be proved what would have been the right policy in 1973. But...you look at the conditions of 1973, in which all of the Arab countries, including Egypt, were considered to be substantially on the Soviet side, in which there were Israeli armies at the outskirts of Cairo and Damascus, in which Western Europe and Japan were suffering and we were suffering from an oil embargo, in which there was a great danger that the war might flare up again and the economic dislocations that already occurred might become unmanageable.

We thought that it was, above all, important to get the peace process started, to deal with those Arab countries that were willing to take a risk for peace, and then as the parties gained confidence in the process of peace, to move toward progressively bolder steps.

If we had put forward a comprehensive scheme — at least that was our judgement under the conditions that then existed — you must remember also the domestic difficulties that existed in the United States at that period. We thought that the danger of its failing would sharpen the embargo, increase Soviet domination of the countries concerned, and enhance the radicalism of the area.

So we thought it was important to take the specific steps that have been taken and that, while of course they have not solved the problem, have given us the time in which to work on a more comprehensive solution.

I think it is now generally agreed, and Israel agrees too, that the time for individual steps with individual countries is probably over and that we now have to work on a wider canvas. And I think, as events in Lebanon have proved, we are still the country toward which most of the parties in the Middle East look for constructive solutions to the problem.

A year or so down the road, whatever disagreement I may have with the distinguished panel of this morning as to the specifics they would put forward in a comprehensive solution, I think the basic strategy will begin to emerge, so we are only really debating whether that strategy should have been adopted in 1973 and whether time was lost or not. I believe that if we had adopted it in 1973 the danger of a blowup would have been outweighed by anything that could have been achieved at that period.

Q: Mr. [George] Chaplin [Vice President of the Society]:
    Mr. Secretary, this morning some of your articulate and presumptuous successors had some comments to make about the Middle East, Russia, and Panama. In your judgment, which of those take priority as overriding problems for this country?
Secretary Kissinger:
    I don't believe that we can really choose among our problems. I

think the relationship between us and the industrial democracies is essential to having a constructive diplomacy; that the relations between us and the Soviet Union are essential for any long-term peace. And I believe that the Middle East is sufficiently explosive so that it could make all other policies fail. And I fear that we cannot set priorities here and that unless we can deal with all of these issues simultaneously, we may not be able to deal with any of them effectively.

VI. The Multipolar-Accommodative Conception: Presentation

President Carter's Address at Commencement Exercises at Notre Dame University, May 22, 1977. Public Papers of the Presidents of the US: Jimmy Carter, 1977 (Book 1 — January 20 to June 24, 1977), pp. 956-962.

...For too many years, we've been willing to adopt the flawed and erroneous principles and tactics of our adversaries, sometimes abandoning our own values for theirs. We've fought fire with fire, never thinking that fire is better quenched with water. This approach failed, with Vietnam the best example of its intellectual and moral poverty. But through failure we have now found the way back to our own principles and values, and we have regained our lost confidence.

By the measure of history, our Nation's 200 years are very brief, and our rise to world eminence is briefer still. It dates from 1945, when Europe and the old international order lay in ruins. Before then, America was largely on the periphery of world affairs. But since then, we have inescapably been at the center of world affairs.

Our policy during this period was guided by two principles: a belief that Soviet expansion was almost inevitable but that it must be contained, and the corresponding belief in the importance of an almost exclusive alliance among non-Communist nations on both sides of the Atlantic. That system could not last forever unchanged. Historical trends have weakened its foundation. The unifying threat of conflict with the Soviet Union has become less intensive, even though the competition has become more extensive....The world is still divided by ideological disputes, dominated by regional conflicts, and threatened by the danger that we will not resolve the differences of race and wealth without violence or without drawing into combat the major military powers. We can no longer separate the traditional issues of war and peace from the new global questions of justice, equity, and human rights.

It is a new world, but America should not fear it. It is a new world, and we should help to shape it. It is a new world that calls for a new American foreign policy — a policy based on constant decency in its values and on optimism in our historical vision.

We can no longer have a policy solely for the industrial nations as the foundation of global stability, but we must respond to the new reality of a politically awakening world.

We can no longer expect that the other 150 nations will follow the dictates of the powerful, but we must continue — confidently — our efforts to inspire, to persuade, and to lead.

Our policy must reflect our belief that the world can hope for more than simple survival and our belief that dignity and freedom are fundamental spiritual requirements. Our policy must shape an international system that will last longer than secret deals.

We cannot make this kind of policy by manipulation. Our policy must be open; it must be candid; it must be one of constructive global involvement....

...Now I believe in detente with the Soviet Union. To me it means progress toward peace. But the effects of detente should not be limited to our own two countries alone....Cooperation also implies obligation. We hope that the Soviet Union will join with us and other nations in playing a larger role in aiding the developing world, for common aid efforts will help us build a bridge of mutual confidence in one another.

...We are taking deliberate steps to improve the chances of lasting peace in the Middle East. Through wide-ranging consultation with leaders of the countries involved — Israel, Syria, Jordan, and Egypt — we have found some areas of agreement and some movement toward consensus. The negotiations must continue.

Through my own public comments, I've also tried to suggest a more flexible framework for the discussion of the three key issues which have so far been so intractable: the nature of a comprehensive peace — what is peace; what does it mean to the Israelis; what does it mean to their Arab neighbors; secondly, the relationship between security and borders — how can the dispute over border delineations be established and settled with a feeling of security on both sides; and the issue of the Palestinian homeland....We will cooperate more closely with the newly influential countries in Latin America, Africa, and Asia. We need their friendship and cooperation in a common effort as the structure of world power changes.

More than 100 years ago, Abraham Lincoln said that our Nation could not exist half slave and half free. We know a peaceful world cannot long exist one-third rich and two-thirds hungry.

Most nations share our faith that, in the long run, expanded and equitable trade will best help the developing countries to help themselves. But the immediate problems of hunger, disease, illiteracy, and repression are here now.

The Western democracies, the OPEC nations, and the developed Communist countries can cooperate through existing international institutions in providing more effective aid. This is an excellent alternative to war.

We have a special need for cooperation and consultation with other nations in this hemisphere — to the north and to the south. We do not need another slogan. Although these are our close friends and neighbors, our links with them are the same links of equality that we forge for the rest of the world. We will be dealing with them as part of a new, world-wide mosaic of global, regional, and bilateral relations....Finally, let me say that we are committed to a peaceful resolution of the crisis in southern Africa. The time has come for the principle of majority rule to be the basis for political order, recognizing that in a democratic system the rights of the minority must also be protected.

To be peaceful, change must come promptly. The Soviet Union is determined to work together with our European allies and with the concerned African States to shape a congenial international framework for the rapid and progressive transformation of southern African society and to help protect it from unwarranted outside interference.

Let me conclude by summarizing: Our policy is based on an historical vision of America's role. Our policy is derived from a larger view of global change. Our policy is rooted in our moral values, which never change. Our policy is reinforced by our material wealth and by our military power. Our policy is designed to serve mankind. And it is a policy that I hope will make you proud to be Americans.

Thank you.

VII. Carter's Collaborative Diplomatic Initiative of 1977, and the Multipolar-Accommodative Conception: Application

Joint US-Soviet Statement on the Middle East, October 1, 1977. *Bulletin,* **Vol. LXXVII, pp. 639-640.**

Having exchanged views regarding the unsafe situation which remains in the Middle East, US Secretary of State Cyrus Vance and Member of the Politbureau of the Central Committee of the CPSU, Minister for Foreign Affairs of the USSR A.A. Gromyko have the following statement to make on behalf of their countries, which are cochairmen of the Geneva Peace Conference on the Middle East.

1. Both governments are convinced that vital interests of the peoples of this area, as well as the interests of strengthening peace and international security in general, urgently dictate the necessity of achieving, as soon as possible, a just and lasting settlement of the Arab-Israeli conflict. This settlement should be comprehensive, incorporating all parties concerned and all questions.

The United States and the Soviet Union believe that, within the framework of a comprehensive settlement of the Middle East problem, all specific questions of the settlement should be resolved, including such key issues as withdrawal of Israeli Armed Forces from territories occupied in the 1967 conflict, the resolution of the Palestinian question, including insuring the legitimate rights of the Palestinian people, termination of the state of war and establishment of normal peaceful relations on the basis of mutual recognition of the principles of sovereignty, territorial integrity, and political independence.

The two governments believe that, in addition to such measures for insuring the security of the borders between Israel and the neighboring Arab states as the establishment of demilitarized zones and the agreed stationing in them of UN troops or observers, international guarantees of such borders as well as of the observance of the terms of the settlement can also be established should the contracting parties so desire. The United States and the

109

Soviet Union are ready to participate in these guarantees, subject to their constitutional processes.

2. The United States and the Soviet Union believe that the only right and effective way for achieving a fundamental solution to all aspects of the Middle East problem in its entirety is negotiations within the framework of the Geneva Peace Conference, specially convened for these purposes, with participation in its work of the representatives of all the parties involved in the conflict including those of the Palestinian people, and legal and contractual formalization of the decisions reached at the conference.

In their capacity as cochairmen of the Geneva Conference, the United States and the USSR affirm their intention, through joint efforts and in their contacts with parties concerned, to facilitate in every way the resumption of the work of the conference not later than December 1977. The cochairmen note that there still exist several questions of a procedural and organizational nature which remain to be agreed upon by the participants to the conference.

3. Guided by the goal of achieving a just political settlement in the Middle East and of eliminating the explosive situation in this area of the world, the United States and the USSR appeal to all the parties in the conflict to understand the necessity for careful consideration of each other's legitimate rights and interests and to demonstrate mutual readiness to act accordingly.

VIII. Carter and the Multipolar-Accommodative Conception: Transformation

State of the Union Address by President Carter before a Joint Session of the Congress on January 23, 1980. *Bulletin,* **Vol. LXXXX, February 1980, pp. A-B.**

The 1980s have been born in turmoil, strife, and change. This is a time of challenge to our interests and our values, and it's a time that tests our wisdom and our skills. At this time in Iran 50 Americans are still held captive, innocent victims of terrorism and anarchy. Also at this moment, massive Soviet troops are attempting to subjugate the fiercely independent and deeply religious people of Afghanistan. These two acts — one of international terrorism and one of military aggression — present a serious challenge to the United States of America and indeed to all the nations of the world. Together, we will meet these threats to peace.

I am determined that the United States will remain the strongest of all nations, but our power will never be used to initiate a threat to the security of any nation or to the rights of any human being. We seek to be and to remain secure — a nation at peace in a stable world. But to be secure we must face the world as it is. Three basic developments have helped to shape our challenges:

★   The steady growth and increased projection of Soviet military power beyond its own borders;

★   The overwhelming dependence of the Western democracies on oil supplies from the Middle East; and

★   The press of social and religious and economic and political change in the many nations of the developing world — exemplified by the revolution in Iran.

Each of these factors is important in its own right. Each interacts with the others. All must be faced together — squarely and courageously.

We will face these challenges. And we will meet them with the best that is in us. And we will not fail....

Now, as during the last three and one-half decades, the relationship between our country — the United States of America — and the Soviet Union is the most critical factor in determining whether the world will live in peace or be engulfed in global conflict.

Since the end of the Second World War, America has led other nations in meeting the challenge of mounting Soviet power. This has not been a simple or a static relationship. Between us there has been cooperation, there has been competition, and at times there has been confrontation....

We superpowers will also have the responsibility to exercise restraint in the use of our great military force. The integrity and the independence of weaker nations must not be threatened. They must know that in our presence they are secure. But now the Soviet Union has taken a radical and an aggressive new step. It's using its great military power against a relatively defenseless nation. The implications of the Soviet invasion of Afghanistan could pose the most serious threat to the peace since the Second World War.

The vast majority of nations on Earth have condemned this latest Soviet attempt to extend its colonial domination of others and have demanded the immediate withdrawal of Soviet troops. The Moslem world is especially and justifiably outraged by this aggression against an Islamic people. No action of a world power has ever been so quickly and so overwhelmingly condemned.

But verbal condemnation is not enough. The Soviet Union must pay a concrete price for their aggression. While this invasion continues, we and the other nations of the world cannot conduct business as usual with the Soviet Union.

That's why the United States has imposed stiff economic sanctions on the Soviet Union.

I will not issue any permits for Soviet ships to fish in the coastal waters of the United States.

I've cut Soviet access to high-technology equipment and to agricultural products.

I've limited other commerce with the Soviet Union, and I've asked our allies and friends to join with us in restraining their own trade with the Soviets and not to replace our own embargoed items.

And I have notified the Olympic Committee that with Soviet invading forces in Afghanistan, neither the American people nor I will support sending an Olympic team to Moscow.

The Soviet Union is going to have to answer some basic questions: Will it help promote a more stable international environment in which its own legitimate, peaceful concerns can be pursued? Or will it continue to expand its military power far beyond its genuine security needs and use that power for colonial conquest?

The Soviet Union must realize that its decision to use military force in Afghanistan will be costly to every political and economic relationship it values.

The region which is now threatened by Soviet troops in Afghanistan is of great strategic importance. It contains more than two-thirds of the world's exportable oil. The Soviet effort to dominate Afghanistan has brought Soviet military forces to within 300 miles of the Indian Ocean and close to the Straits of Hormuz — a waterway through which most of the world's oil must flow. The Soviet Union is now attempting to consolidate a strategic position, therefore, that poses a grave threat to the free movement of Middle East oil.

This situation demands careful thought, steady nerves, and resolute action, not only for this year but for many years to come. It demands collective efforts to meet this new threat to security in the Persian Gulf and in southwest Asia. It demands the participation of all those who rely on oil from the Middle East and who are concerned with global peace and stability. And it demands consultation and close cooperation with countries in the area which might be threatened.

Meeting this challenge will take national will, diplomatic and political wisdom, economic sacrifice, and, of course, military capability. We must call on the best that is in us to preserve the security of this crucial region.

Let our position be absolutely clear: An attempt by any outside force to gain control of the Persian Gulf region will be regarded as an assault on the vital interests of the United States of America, and such an assault will be repelled by any means necessary, including military force....

We've increased and strengthened our naval presence in the Indian Ocean, and we are now making arrangements for key naval and air facilities to be used by our forces in the region of northeast Africa and the Persian Gulf....The United States will take action — consistent with our laws — to assist Pakistan in resisting any outside aggression. And I'm asking the Congress specifically to reaffirm this agreement. I'm also working, along with the leaders of other nations, to provide additional military and economic aid for Pakistan. That request will come to you in just a few days.

In the weeks ahead, we will further strengthen political and military ties with other nations in the region....Finally, we are prepared to work with other countries in the region to share a cooperative security framework that respects differing values and political beliefs, yet which enhances the independence, security, and prosperity of all.

All these efforts combined emphasize our dedication to defend and preserve the vital interests of the region and of the nation which we represent, and those of our allies in Europe and the Pacific and also in the parts of the world which have such great strategic importance to us, stretching especially through the Middle East and southwest Asia. With your help, I will pursue these efforts with vigor and with determination. You and I will act as necessary to protect and to preserve our nation's security.

IX. Counterpoint: The Soviet Conception of a Middle East Settlement

Text of the Soviet proposal, presented on October 4, 1976 to the governments of the US, Syria, Jordan and Israel. Quoted from Radio Moscow by Sella, *Soviet Political and Military Conduct,* **pp. 162-164.**

The problem of a Middle East settlement is a particularly urgent one among the complicated international issues that need to be solved in the interests of maintaining and strengthening peace. Tensions are not abating in the Middle East. The situation in that region is extremely unsound and unstable. There could be a new military explosion there at any moment. The peoples of the Middle East countries are living in unstable conditions that constantly jeopardise their safety. They are deprived of opportunities to devote their efforts to peaceful construction and the improvement of their living conditions. Attempts are made to keep the Arab people of Palestine in the position of a banished people.

The entire course of events in the Middle East during the past few years points to one thing — there cannot and will not be peace in the region until the removal of the causes of the Middle East conflict: Israel's occupation of Arab territories, the deprivation of the Arab people of Palestine of their inalienable rights, and the continued state of war. One should not hope that the elimination of one or another hotbed of military conflict will be enough to restore peace to the Middle East.

The tragic events in Lebanon are a clear confirmation of this. The Lebanese crisis could not have happened if a comprehensive political settlement had been achieved in the Middle East. It would also obviously be easier to solve the problems which are tearing this small Middle East country apart if such a settlement existed or if serious efforts were being made to reach it.

Only those who are making efforts to preserve the status quo in the Middle East for the sake of their narrow purposes can protest against a broad political settlement and oppose its achievement.

In the view of the Soviet Union, the situation that is developing in the Middle East requires urgent efforts to ensure a turn away from war to peace in the area. The Soviet Union has already suggested that the work of the Geneva Middle East peace conference should be resumed for this purpose. This is precisely the kind of forum that is recognised as politically acceptable by all the sides involved. Concerned as it is with the dangerous state of affairs in the Middle East, the Soviet Union now again urges the sides immediately involved in the Middle East conflict, all participants in the Geneva peace conference, to resume its work. As for the Soviet side, it would be ready to take part in the work of the conference in October-November 1976.

The practice of international negotiations and conferences shows that an important ingredient in success is the precise determination of a range of questions to be discussed by delegates. When these questions have been formulated and are in front of the participants in the talks, the prospects for coming to the necessary agreements become clearer.

The Soviet Union is guided by a desire to accelerate achievement of a Middle East settlement and, with this aim in mind, to assist with the resumption of the Geneva peace conference. That is why it has made the following proposal for the conference agenda to be discussed by the participants:

(1)   The withdrawal of Israeli troops from all Arab territories occupied in 1967.

(2)   The exercise by the Arab people of Palestine of their inalienable rights, including their right to self-determination and the establishment of their own State.

(3)   The ensurance of the right to independent existence and security for all states immediately involved in the conflict — the Arab states neighbouring Israel, on the one side, and the State of Israel, on the other — with appropriate international guarantees offered to them.

(4)   The ending of the state of war between the Arab countries concerned and Israel.

It is the Soviet view that the proposed agenda covers all the key aspects of a settlement. It takes into account the legitimate rights and interests of all sides immediately involved in the conflict — the Arab states, the Arab people of Palestine and the State of Israel.

As for the organisation of work at the Geneva peace conference, the Soviet Union has already urged that this should be done in two stages. The Palestine Liberation Organisation must obviously take part in the work of the conference on an equal footing from the very outset.

The conference agenda could be co-ordinated fully at the initial preparatory stage and the order of discussion of concrete aspects of a settlement could be determined. The second stage of the conference could concentrate on hammering out essential agreements. The conference must end in the adoption of a final document...having the nature of an agreement.

The Soviet Union is confident that a practical opportunity exists of eliminating the basic causes of the Middle East conflict and of agreeing on a comprehensive settlement. It is ready to continue its persistent efforts to achieve this, together with all other participants in the Geneva peace conference.

Notes

Chapter 1

1 John Lewis Gaddis, *Strategies of Containment: A Critical Appraisal of Postwar American National Security Policy* (New York: Oxford University Press, 1982), p. ix.
2 Ole R. Holsti, "Foreign Policy Formation Viewed Cognitively," in Robert Axelrod, ed., *Structure of Decision: The Cognitive Maps of Political Elites* (Princeton: Princeton University Press, 1976), pp. 33-34; Alexander L. George, "The Causal Nexus Between Cognitive Beliefs and Decision-Making Behavior: The 'Operational Code' Belief System," in Lawrence S. Falkowski, ed., *Psychological Models in International Politics* (Boulder: Westview Press, 1979), pp. 104-109.
3 George, "The Causal Nexus," p. 109.
4 Holsti, "Foreign Policy Formation Viewed Cognitively," p. 34.
5 Robert Jervis, *Perception and Misperception in International Politics* (Princeton: Princeton University Press, 1976), pp. 117-202; 288-315. See also Richard Smoke, *War: Controlling Escalation* (Cambridge: Harvard University Press, 1977), pp. 284-286; Michael Brecher, *The Foreign Policy System of Israel: Setting, Images, Process* (New Haven: Yale University Press, 1972), pp. 11-12.
6 Loch K. Johnson, "Operational Codes and the Prediction of Leadership Behavior: Senator Frank Church at Mid-career," in Margaret G. Hermann, ed., *A Psychological Examination of Political Leaders* (New York: The Free Press, 1977), p. 89. See also Glenn H. Snyder and Paul Diesing, *Conflict Among Nations: Bargaining, Decision Making and System Structure in International Crises* (Princeton: Princeton University Press, 1977), pp. 331-338.
7 Address by Leonid Brezhnev, September 15, 1982, in Yehuda Lukacs, ed., *Documents on the Israeli-Palestinian Conflict, 1967-1983* (New York: Cambridge University Press, 1985), pp. 14-15. See also Bernard Reich, *Quest for Peace: United States-Israeli Relations and the Arab-Israeli Conflict* (New Brunswick: Transaction Books, 1977), p. 101; Amnon Sella, *Soviet Political and Military Conduct in the Middle East* (London: Macmillan, 1981), p. 33. For a detailed exposition of the Soviet position see Appendix IX.
8 Richard M. Nixon, *The Memoirs of Richard Nixon* (New York: Grosset and Dunlap, 1978), p. 885.
9 Stanley Hoffmann, *Gulliver's Troubles: Or the Setting of American Foreign Policy* (New York: McGraw-Hill, 1968), pp. 190-194. See also Michael Roskin, "From Pearl Harbor to Vietnam: Shifting Generational Paradigms and Foreign Policy," *Political Science Quarterly* 89 (Fall 1974), pp. 565-573; Samuel P. Huntington, *American Politics: The Promise of Disharmony* (Cambridge, Mass: Harvard University Press, 1981), pp. 142-149.
10 President Nixon News Conference of January 27, 1969. Quoted in Bernard Reich, "The Evolution of United States Policy in the Arab-Israeli Zone," *Middle East Review* 9 (Spring 1977), p. 13.
11 Gerald A. Combs, *Nationalist, Realist, and Radical: Three Views of American Diplomacy* (New York: Harper & Row 1972), pp. 3, 25.
12 Snyder and Diesing, *Conflict Among Nations*, pp. 297-299. See also Charles Lockhart, "Problems in the Management and Resolution of International Con-

flicts," *World Politics* XXIV (April 1977), p. 381; and Abraham Ben-Zvi, "In Pursuit of National Security: A Juxtaposition of American Images and Policies," *The Journal of Strategic Studies* IV (December 1981), pp. 386-387.

13   Snyder and Diesing, *Conflict Among Nations*, pp. 297-299.

14   *Ibid.*, pp. 335-337.

15   *Ibid.*

16   Ben-Zvi, "In Pursuit of National Security," p. 388.

17   Snyder and Diesing, *Conflict Among Nations*, p. 309.

Chapter 2

1   Ole R. Holsti, "The Three-Headed Eagle: The United States and System Change," *International Studies Quarterly* XXIII (September 1979), p. 343; Daniel Yergin, *Shattered Peace: The Origins of the Cold War and the National Security State* (Boston: Houghton Mifflin, 1977), p. 11; Alexander Dallin and Gail W. Lapidus, "Reagan and the Russians: United States Policy Toward the Soviet Union and Eastern Europe," in Kenneth A. Oye, Robert J. Lieber and Donald Rothchild, eds., *Eagle Defiant: US Foreign Policy in the 1980s* (Boston: Little, Brown, 1982), p. 206; William Schneider, "Conservatism, Not Interventionism: Trends in Foreign Policy Opinion, 1974-1982," in *Eagle Defiant*, p. 50. See also William Zimmerman, "Rethinking Soviet Foreign Policy: Changing American Perspectives," *International Journal* XXXV (Summer 1980), pp. 551-552; and Charles Krauthammer, "The Poverty of Realism," *The New Republic* 194 (February 17, 1986), pp. 14-22; see in particular his analysis of the neo-internationalist orientation.

2   Yergin, *Shattered Peace*, p. 194.

3   *Ibid.*, p. 196; Daniel Pipes, "Breaking All the Rules: American Debate Over the Middle East," *International Security* 9 (Fall 1984), p. 125.

4   Shmuel Sandler, "Linkage and Decoupling in American Foreign Policy," in Nissan Oren, ed., *When Patterns Change: Turning Points in International Politics* (New York: St. Martin's Press, 1984), pp. 155-161. See also Robert L. Beisner, "1898 and 1968: The Anti-Imperialists and the Doves," *Political Science Quarterly* 95 (June 1970), p. 211.

5   Holsti, "The Three-Headed Eagle," p. 34. See also Robert H. Johnson, "Exaggerating America's Stakes in Third World Conflicts," *International Security* 10 (Winter 1985/86), pp. 39-40.

6   Ernst B. Hass, "On Hedging Our Bets: Selective Engagement with the Soviet Union," in Aaron Wildavsky, ed., *Beyond Containment: Alternative American Policies Toward the Soviet Union* (San Francisco: Institute for Contemporary Studies, 1983), pp. 99-100. See also Robert W. Tucker, "Containment and the Search for Alternatives: A Critique," in *Beyond Containment*, pp. 70-71; Ernest R. May, *"Lessons" of the Past: The Use and Misuse of History in American Foreign Policy* (New York: Oxford University Press, 1973), pp. 75-84; Richard Ned Lebow, "Generational Learning and Conflict Management," *International Security* XL (Autumn 1985), pp. 565-567.

7   Yergin, *Shattered Peace*, p. 11; Holsti, "The Three-Headed Eagle," pp. 343-345; Lloyd C. Gardner, "Truman Era Foreign Policy: Recent Historical Trends," in Richard S. Kirkendall, ed., *The Truman Period as a Research Field: A Reappraisal*

1972 (Columbia, Missouri: University of Missouri Press, 1974), pp. 66; Lebow, "Generational Learning," p. 567.

8 Raymond L. Garthoff, *Detente and Confrontation: American-Soviet Relations from Nixon to Reagan* (Washington DC: The Brookings Institution, 1985), p. 674. The distinction between the local and global perspectives is based on Sandler, "Linkage and Decoupling," p. 156; and Peter Mangold, *Superpower Intervention in the Middle East* (London: Croom Helm, 1978), p. 190. See also Alan Dowty, *Middle East Crisis: U.S. Decision-Making in 1958, 1970, and 1973* (Berkeley: University of California Press, 1984), p. 57.

9 Dallin and Lapidus, "Reagan and the Russians," pp. 197, 209. See also William Welch, *American Images of Soviet Foreign Policy* (New Haven: Yale University Press, 1970), p. 61.

10 Dallin and Lapidus, "Reagan and the Russians," p. 209; James N. Rosenau and Ole R. Holsti, "US Leadership in a Shrinking World: The Breakdown of Consensus and the Emergence of Conflicting Belief Systems," *World Politics* XXXV (April 1983), p. 378; Haas, "On Hedging Our Bets," pp. 99-100; William D. Anderson and Sterling J. Kernek, "How 'Realist' is Reagan's Diplomacy?" *Political Science Quarterly* 100 (Fall 1985), pp. 333-392; R. Garthoff, *Detente and Confrontation*, pp. 35-112.

11 Address by Jeane Kirkpatrick, US Representative to the United Nations, to the Uruguayan National War College in Montevideo on August 4, 1981. *Official Text*, August 10, 1981 (published by United States Information Service). See also Nimrod Novik, *Encounter with Reality: Reagan and the Middle East* (the First Term) (Boulder: Westview Press, 1985), p. 22.

12 *Time*, February 9, 1981.

13 Alexander M. Haig, Jr., *Caveat: Realism, Reagan, and Foreign Policy* (New York: Macmillan, 1984), pp. 29-31.

14 Dallin and Lapidus, "Reagan and the Russians," pp. 210.

15 Statement by Matthew Nimetz, quoted in Ben-Zvi, "In Pursuit of National Security," p. 409.

16 Address by Secretary of State Haig, May 24, 1981. Quoted in Garthoff, *Detente and Confrontation*, p. 1050. See also Lebow, "Generational Learning," p. 572.

17 Samuel P. Huntington, "Renewed Hostility," in Joseph S. Nye, Jr., ed., *The Making of America's Soviet Policy* (New Haven: Yale University Press, 1984), p. 284. See also Dallin and Lapidus, "Reagan and the Russians," p. 210; Barry Rubin, "The Reagan Administration and the Middle East," in *Eagle Defiant*, pp. 374-375; Robert W. Tucker, "The Middle East: Carterism Without Carter," *Commentary* 69 (September 1981), p. 31.

18 Blema S. Steinberg, "American Foreign Policy in the Middle East: A Study in Changing Priorities," in Janice Gross Stein, ed., *Crossroads: Regional Forces and External Powers* (Oakville, Ontario: Mosaic Press, 1983), pp. 113, 141. See also Abraham Ben-Zvi, "The Limits of Detente: Henry Kissinger and U.S. Middle East Policy in Retrospect," *Co-existence* 15 (1978), p. 101; *idem*, "Middle East Flashback, 1950-1976," *Midstream* XXII (December 1976), pp. 6-7; Ann Schultz, "United States Policy in the Middle East," *Current History* 68 (February 1975), p. 54.

19 Statement of Richard Burt, Director of the Bureau of Political-Military Affairs at the US State Department, before the Subcommittee on International Security and Scientific Affairs of the House of Representatives, March 23, 1981. *Official Text*, March 25, 1981, p. 3. See also, in this connection: John H. Sigler, "United States Policy in the Aftermath of Lebanon: The Perils of Unilateralism," *International Journal* XXXVIII (Autumn 1983), p. 557.

20 Secretary of Defense Caspar W. Weinberger interviewed on the CBS television program "Face the Nation," March 8, 1981. See also Haig, *Caveat*, p. 321; Bernard Reich, *The United States and Israel: Influence in the Special Relationship* (New York: Praeger, 1984), p. 91, and Haim Shaked, "Change in the Middle East: Is There a Chance for Peace?" in Harry S. Allen and Ivan Volgyes, eds., *Israel, the Middle East, and U.S. Interests* (New York: Praeger, 1983), p. 32.

21 Ben-Zvi, "Middle East Flashback," pp. 6-7; William B. Quandt, "United States in the Middle East: Constraints and Choices," in Paul J. Hammond and Sidney S. Alexander, eds., *Political Systems in the Middle East* (New York: American Elsevier, 1972), p. 501; P.M. Dadant, "American and Soviet Defence Systems vis-à-vis the Middle East," in Willard A. Beling, ed., *The Middle East: Quest for an American Policy* (New York: State University of New York Press, 1975), p. 174; William R. Polk, *The United States and the Arab World* (Cambridge, Mass: Harvard University Press, 1975), pp. 373-374; Steinberg, "American Foreign Policy in the Middle East," p. 113.

22 Statement by Burt, March 23, 1981, p. 3.

23 Abraham Ben-Zvi, *Alliance Politics and the Limits of Influence: The Case of the US and Israel, 1975-1983* (Tel-Aviv: Jaffee Center for Strategic Studies and Boulder: Westview Press, 1984), p. 33. See also Karen Dawisha, "The USSR in the Middle East: Superpower in Eclipse?" *Foreign Affairs* 61 (Winter 82-83), p. 442.

24 Dallin and Lapidus, "Reagan and the Russians," p. 210.

25 *Ibid*; Shai Feldman, *The Reagan Administration and Israel: The Second Term* (Tel-Aviv: Jaffee Center for Strategic Studies, 1985) (Hebrew), pp. 12-15; Huntington, "Renewed Hostility," p. 289.

26 *Official Text*, January 31, 1985. See also, in this connection, Tucker, "Containment and the Search for Alternatives," pp. 71, 75.

27 President Reagan's News Conference of February 21, 1985, *New York Times*, February 22, 1985; *Davar* (Hebrew), February 22, 1985.

28 Quoted in *The Washington Post*, February 15, 1985.

29 Alexander L. George, "Crisis Prevention Reexamined," in *idem, Managing U.S.-Soviet Rivalry: Problems of Crisis Prevention* (Boulder: Westview Press, 1983), pp. 376-377. See also Yair Evron, "Great Powers' Military Intervention in the Middle East," in Milton Leitenberg and Gabriel Sheffer, eds., *Great Power Intervention in the Middle East* (New York: Pergamon Press, 1979), pp. 22-23.

30 Secretary Shultz's News Conference, May 31, 1985. *Official Text*, May 31, 1985. See also *Backgrounder* (published by USIS), May 30, 1985; *Ha'aretz* (Hebrew), June 2, 1985.

31 George W. Breslauer, "Why Detente Failed: An Interpretation," in *Managing U.S.-Soviet Rivalry*, p. 330. See also Carsten Hollbraad, *Superpowers and International Conflict* (New York: St. Martin Press, 1979), p. 10; *idem.*, "Condominium and Concert," in *Superpowers and World Order* (Canberra: Australian National University Press, 1971), pp. 3-4.

32 Holbraad, *Superpowers and International Conflict*, p. 2.

33 Stanley Hoffmann, *Primacy or World Order: American Foreign Policy Since the Cold War* (New York: McGraw-Hill, 1978), p. 44.

34 Henry A. Kissinger, *White House Years* (Boston: Little, Brown, 1979), p. 129.

35 *Ibid*. See also Sandler, "Linkage and Decoupling," pp. 155, 157; Stanley Hoffmann, *Dead Ends: American Foreign Policy in the New Cold War* (New York: Ballinger, 1983), p. 83; Dowty, *Middle East Crisis*, p. 115.

36 Hoffmann, *Dead Ends*, p. 91. See also Robert S. Litwak, *Detente and the Nixon*

121

Doctrine: American Foreign Policy and the Pursuit of Stability, 1969-1976
(Cambridge: Cambridge University Press, 1984), 77-83, 145, 191; Harvey Starr, "The
Kissinger Years: Studying Individuals and Foreign Policy," *International Studies
Quarterly* 24 (December 1980), pp. 487-490.

37 Garthoff, *Detente and Confrontation*, p. 674. See also Dan Handel, *The Process
of Priority Formulation* (Boulder: Westview Press, 1977), pp. 336-337; Hedley Bull,
"Kissinger: The Primacy of Geopolitics," *International Affairs* 56 (1980), p. 486.

38 Gaddis, *Strategies of Containment*, pp. 276-277. See also Dallin and Lapidus,
"Reagan and the Russians," p. 206; Schneider, "Conservatism, Not Interventionism," p. 41; Ishaq I. Ghanyem and Alden H. Voth, *The Kissinger Legacy: American
Middle East Policy* (New York: Praeger, 1985), pp. 159-161; Zimmerman, "Rethinking Soviet Foreign Policy," pp. 551-552.

39 Gaddis, *Strategies of Containment*, pp. 58-59.

40 Hoffmann, *Primacy or World Order*, p. 43.

41 Gaddis, *Strategies of Containment*, pp. 30. See also Litwak, *Detente and the
Nixon Doctrine*, p. 193.

42 Henry A. Kissinger, *Years of Upheaval* (Boston: Little, Brown, 1982). p. 299. See
also Garthoff, *Detente and Confrontation*, p. 365.

43 George, "Crisis Prevention Reexamined," p. 385. See also Blema S. Steinberg,
"Superpower Conceptions of Peace in the Middle East," *The Jerusalem Journal of
International Relations* 2 (Summer 1977), p. 69.

44 Kissinger, *White House Years*, pp. 161-162. See also Douglas Stuard and Harvey
Starr, "The 'Inherent Bad Faith Model' Reconsidered: Dulles, Kennedy, and
Kissinger," *Political Psychology* 3 (Fall/Winter 1981-82), p. 13; Dallin and Lapidus,
"Reagan and the Russians," p. 297; Litwak, *Detente and the Nixon Doctrine*, pp.
164-165.

45 David Vital, *The Survival of Small States: Studies in Small Power/Great Power
Conflict* (London: Oxford University Press, 1972), pp. 90-91.

46 Alexander L. George, "Domestic Constraints on Regime Change in US Foreign
Policy: The Need for Policy Legitimacy," in Ole R. Holsti, Randolph M. Siverson, and
Alexander L. George, eds., *Change in the International System* (Boulder: Westview
Press, 1980), pp. 252-253; Stanley Hoffmann, "Detente," in *The Making of
America's Soviet Policy*, p. 232; Steven L. Spiegel, *The Other Arab-Israeli Conflict:
Making America's Middle East Policy, From Truman to Reagan* (Chicago: The
University of Chicago Press, 1985), p. 172; Alan Dowty, "The Impact of the 1973 War
on the U.S. Approach to the Middle East," in *When Patterns Change, p. 254.*

47 Secretary Kissinger's News Conference of November 12, 1973, *Department of
State Bulletin* LXIX, p. 716. See also Garthoff, *Detente and Confrontation*, p. 30;
Litwak, *Detente and the Nixon Doctrine*, p. 83.

48 Gaddis, *Strategies of Containment*, pp. 289; Alexander L. George, "Detente:
The Search for a 'Constructive' Relationship," in *Managing US Soviet Rivalry*, p. 20;
Harvey Starr, "The Kissinger Years: Studying Individuals and Foreign Policy,"
International Studies Quarterly 24 (December 1980), pp. 489-492, Litwak, *Detente
and the Nixon Doctrine*, p. 90.

49 Hoffmann, "Detente," p. 238. See also George, "Domestic Constraints on
Regime Change," p. 252; Paul Seabury, "Reinspecting Containment," in *Beyond
Containment*, p. 45; Gaddis, *Strategies of Containment*, pp. 289; Ghanayem and
Voth, *The Kissinger Legacy*, p. 161; Garthoff, *Detente and Confrontation*, p. 30.

50 Statement of Secretary Kissinger, September 19, 1974. *Bulletin* LXXI, p. 508.

Parts of this statement are reprinted in Appendix III. See also *idem, American Foreign Policy* (third edition) (New York: Norton, 1977), p. 303; Spiegel, *The Other Arab-Israeli Conflict*, p. 172; Marshall Goldman and Raymond Vernon, "Economic Relations," in *The Making of America's Soviet Policy*, pp. 162-164; Garthoff, *Detente and Confrontation*, p. 1050; *idem*, "American-Soviet Relations in Perspective," *Political Science Quarterly* 100 (Winter 1985/86), p. 545.

51   Garthoff, *Detente and Confrontation*, p. 31. See also Nixon, *Memoirs*, p. 346; Hoffmann, *Primacy or World Power*, p. 46; Litwak, *Detente and the Nixon Doctrine*, pp. 110-111.

52   Breslauer, "Why Detente Failed," p. 326; George, "Detente: The Search for a 'Constructive' Relationship," p. 21; Corall Ball, *The Diplomacy of Detente: The Kissinger Era* (New York: St. Martin's Press, 1977), p. 30.

53   Kissinger, *White House Years*, pp. 143-144. See also Garthoff, *Detente and Confrontation*, p. 292; *idem*, "Containment: Its Past and Future," *International Security* 5 (Spring 1981), p. 82; James Chase, *A World Elsewhere: The New American Foreign Policy* (New York: Charles Scribner's Sons, 1973), p. 42; Garthoff, *Detente and Confrontation*, pp. 31-32.

54   Statement of Secretary Kissinger, September 19, 1974, *Bulletin* LXXI, p. 508. See also Garthoff, *Detente and Confrontation*, p. 32.

55   Nixon, *Memoirs*, p. 316. See also Hoffmann, *Dead Ends*, p. 69; Litwak, *Detente and the Nixon Doctrine*, p. 110.

56   Gaddis, *Strategies of Containment*, p. 291. See also Hoffmann, "Detente," p. 237; Kissinger, *Years of Upheaval*, p. 239.

57   George, "Crisis Prevention Reexamined," p. 388. See also Huntington, "Renewed Hostility," p. 270.

58   Snyder and Diesing, *Conflict Among Nations*, p. 446.

59   Kissinger, *Years of Upheaval*, p. 204, emphasis original. See also Matti Golan, *The Secret Conversations of Henry Kissinger: Step-by-Step Diplomacy in the Middle East* (New York: Quadrangle, 1976), p. 173; Tucker, "Containment and the Search for Alternatives," p. 71; Chase, *A World Elsewhere*, pp. 48-49; Garthoff, *Detente and Confrontation*, p. 129.

60   John G. Stoessinger, *Henry Kissinger: The Anguish of Power* (New York: Norton, 1976), p. 101.

61   Kissinger, *White House Years*, pp. 341-352; Alexander L. George, "Missed Opportunities for Crisis Prevention: The War of Attrition and Angola," in *Managing U.S.-Soviet Rivalry*, p. 189.

62   Kissinger, *White House Years*, p. 352. See also Spiegel, *The Other Arab-Israeli Conflict*, pp. 176, 182.

63   Quoted in Spiegel, *The Other Arab-Israeli Conflict*, p. 1983. See also *The New York Times*, July 3, 1970; Dowty, *Middle East Crisis*, pp. 115-116.

64   Address by Secretary Kissinger, September 16, 1975, *Bulletin* LXXIII, p. 497. Emphasis added. Parts of this address are reprinted in Appendix IV. See also George, "Missed Opportunities for Crisis Prevention," p. 189; Janice Gross Stein, "War Termination and Conflict Reduction or How Wars Should End," *The Jerusalem Journal of International Relations* 1 (Fall 1975), pp. 20-21; Adam M. Garfinkle, "'Common Sense' About Middle East Diplomacy: Implications for U.S. Policy in the Near Term," *Middle East Review* 17 (Winter 1984/1985), p. 29.

65   Robert W. Tucker, "The Middle East: The View from Washington," in Nissan Oren, ed., *Images and Reality in International Politics* (New York: St. Martin Press,

1984), p. 215. See also Spiegel, *The Other Arab-Israeli Conflict*, p. 224; Steinberg, "American Foreign Policy in the Middle East," pp. 120-121.

66 Address by Secretary Kissinger, September 23, 1974, *Bulletin* LXXI, pp. 499-500. See also Address by Henry Kissinger, July 27, 1976, *idem*, LXXV, p. 236; and Secretary Kissinger's News Conference of March 26, 1974, *ibid.*, LXX, p. 463.

67 Janice Gross Stein, "The Alchemy of Peacemaking: The Prerequisites and Corequisites of Progress in the Arab-Israeli Conflict," *International Journal* XXXVIII (Autumn 1983), p. 548. See also Seymour M. Hersh, *The Price of Power: Kissinger in the Nixon White House* (New York: Summit Books, 1983), pp. 630-632.

68 Spiegel, *The Other Arab-Israeli Conflict*, p. 224. See also Ben-Zvi, "The Limits of Detente," p. 115; Address by Secretary Kissinger, September 23, 1974, *Bulletin* LXXI, p. 499; Roger J. Fisher, "Fractionating Conflict," in *idem*, ed., *International Conflict and Behavioral Science* (New York: Basic Books, 1964), p. 105.

69 Ben-Zvi, "The Limits of Detente," pp. 115-116.

70 Secretary Kissinger's News Conference of June 6, 1974, *Bulletin* LXXI, p. 711. Emphasis added.

71 Secretary Kissinger's statement of May 3, 1976, *ibid.* LXXIV, p. 571.

72 *Ibid.*, pp. 359, 559, 1247, 1288; Robert O. Freedman, *Soviet Policy Toward the Middle East Since 1970* (New York: Praeger, 1978), pp. 126, 278-279.

73 George, "Detente: The Search for a 'Constructive' Relationship," p. 24; Seth P. Tillman, *The United States in the Middle East: Interests and Obstacles* (Bloomington: Indiana University Press, 1982), p. 232.

74 Kissinger, *White House Years*, pp. 347, 351, 1254-1255. See also *idem, Years of Upheaval*, p. 202.

75 Edward R.F. Sheehan, "Step by Step in the Middle East," *Foreign Policy*, no. 22 (Spring 1976), p. 18.

76 Breslauer, "Why Detente Failed," p. 327; George, "Detente: The Search for a 'Constructive' Relationship," p. 24; William B. Quandt, *Decade of Decision: American Policy Toward the Arab-Israeli Conflict, 1967-1976* (Berkeley: University of California Press, 1977), p. 211; Dowty, "The Impact of the 1973 War," p. 259; Shlomo Aronson, *Conflict and Bargaining in the Middle East: An Israeli Perspective* (Baltimore: Johns Hopkins University Press, 1978), pp. 200-201; Litwak, *Detente and the Nixon Doctrine*, p. 159.

77 Kissinger, *Years of Upheaval*, p. 594. The text of the "Carter Doctrine" speech is reprinted in Appendix VIII.

78 Hoffmann, "Detente," pp. 242-243. Emphasis added. See also Breslauer, "Why Detente Failed," p. 327; George, "Detente: The Search for a 'Constructive' Relationship," p. 24.

79 Kissinger, *Years of Upheaval*, p. 645. See also Alfred L. Atherton, Jr., "The Soviet Role in the Middle East: An American View," *The Middle East Journal* 39 (Autumn 1985), p. 701.

80 Alexander L. George, "The Arab-Israeli War of October 1973: Origins and Impact," in *Managing US-Soviet Rivalry*, p. 149; Quandt, *Decade of Decisions*, p. 213; Alvin Z. Rubinstein, "Soviet-American Rivalry in the Middle East," *Middle East Review* 9 (Spring 1977), p. 36.

81 Kissinger, *American Foreign Policy*, pp. 133-136. Emphasis added.

82 Secretary Kissinger's News Conference of December 24, 1973, *Bulletin* LXIX, p. 759.

83 *Bulletin* LXX, p. 700. Emphasis added. See also Hoffmann, *Detente*, p. 245.

84 Kissinger, *White House Years*, p. 1254.

85 *Idem, Years of Upheaval*, p. 594.

86 *Ibid.*, p. 1034. Emphasis added.

87 *Ibid.*

88 Atherton, "The Soviet Role in the Middle East," p. 703.

89 Secretary Kissinger's News Conference of September 9, 1975, *Bulletin* LXX, p. 472. See also Abraham S. Becker, "Moscow and the Middle East: A Role for Soviet Guarantees?" *Middle East Review* 8 (1976), p. 52.

90 George, "The Arab-Israeli War of October 1973," p. 149. See also Lawrence L. Whetten, "The Arab-Israeli Dispute: Great Power Behavior," in Gregory Treverton, ed., *Crisis-Management and the Super-powers in the Middle East* (London: The International Institute for Strategic Studies, 1981), p. 77; Kissinger, *Years of Upheaval*, p. 615.

91 Quoted by Sheehan, "Step by Step in the Middle East," pp. 51-52.

92 George, "Political Crises," in *The Making of America's Soviet Policy*, p. 145.

93 Secretary Kissinger's News Conference of October 25, 1973, *Bulletin* LXIX, pp. 586-587. Emphasis added. See also Garthoff, *Detente and Confrontation*, pp. 376-377; Raymord Cohen, *International Politics: The Rules of the Game* (London: Longman, 1981), pp. 101-112; Christopher C. Shoemaker and John Spanier, *Patron-Client State Relationships: Multilateral Crises in the Nuclear Age* (New York: Praeger, 1984), pp. 170-171. The paragraph from Brezhnev's October 24 message is quoted from Kissinger, *Years of Upheaval*, p. 583. For the American reply to Brezhnev see p. 591.

94 Secretary Kissinger's News Conference of December 27, 1973, *Bulletin* LXX, p. 50.

95 Secretary Kissinger interviewed in *US News and World Report*, June 23, 1975. See also Reich, *The United States and Israel*, p. 31.

96 Kissinger, *Years of Upheaval*, p. 615.

97 Saadia Touval, *The Peace Brokers: Mediators in the Arab-Israeli Conflict, 1948-1979* (Princeton: Princeton University Press, 1982), p. 272.

98 Kissinger, *Years of Upheaval*, pp. 204-231; George, "The Arab-Israeli War," p. 143; Galia Golan, "The Arab-Israeli Conflict in Soviet-US Relations," in Yaacov Ro'i, ed., *The Limits of Power: Soviet Policy in the Middle East* (London: Croom Helm, 1979), pp. 8-15; Adam B. Ulam, *Dangerous Relations: The Soviet Union in World Politics, 1970-1982* (New York: Oxford University Press, 1983), p. 119.

99 Alexander L. George, "The Basic Principles Agreement of 1972: Origins and Expectations," in *Managing US Soviet Rivalry*, pp. 110, 114; Galia Golan, *The Yom Kippur War and After: The Soviet Union and the Middle East Crisis* (New York: Cambridge University Press, 1977), p. 227.

100 Secretary Kissinger's News Conference of January 21, 1975, *Bulletin* LXXII, p. 124.

101 Dowty, "The Impact of the 1973 War," p. 260. See also Garthoff, *Detente and Confrontation*, p. 470.

102 Kissinger, *Years of Upheaval*, pp. 1022, 1034; Alvin Z. Rubinstein, *Red Star on the Nile* (Princeton: Princeton University Press, 1977), p. 324; Robert O. Freedman, "The Soviet Conception of a Middle East Peace Settlement," in *The Limits of Power*, pp. 302-303; Karen Dawisha, *Soviet Foreign Policy Towards Egypt* (New York: St. Martins Press, 1979), pp. 77-82; 130; Atherton, "The Soviet Role in the Middle East," p. 703; Garthoff, *Detente and Confrontation*, p. 414; Moshe Zak, "An International

Conference on the Middle East," *The Jerusalem Quarterly* 137 (1986), p. 23.

103 The Soviet Union similarly had limited leverage over its local allies and clients. See, for example, George, "The Arab-Israeli War of October 1973," pp. 143-144; George W. Breslauer, "Soviet Policy in the Middle East, 1967-1972: Unalterable Antagonism or Collaborative Competition?" in *Managing US-Soviet Rivalry*, p. 86.

104 Theodore Draper, "The United States and Israel: Tilt in the Middle East?" *Commentary* 59 (April 1979), p. 31. See also Rubinstein, "Soviet-American Rivalry," p. 36.

105 Spiegel, *The Other Arab-Israeli Conflict*, pp. 268-269.

106 Kissinger, *Years of Upheaval*, p. 749. See also Seyom Brown, *The Crisis of Power* (New York: Columbia University Press, 1979), pp. 102-103; Sella, *Soviet Political and Military Conduct*, p. 107.

107 Stein, "The Alchemy of Peacemaking," pp. 547-548. See also Touval, *The Peace Brokers*, p. 243.

108 Tucker, "The Middle East," p. 215. See also Edward R.F. Sheehan, *The Arabs, Israelis, and Kissinger* (New York: Thomas Y. Crowell, 1976), pp. 16-17; Ben-Zvi, *"The Limits of Detente," pp. 113-116;* Henry Kissinger, *For the Record* (Boston: Little, Brown, 1977), p. 107 (reprinted from an essay in *Time*, January 2, 1978).

Chapter 3

1 Holsti, "The Three-Headed Eagle," pp. 346-348; Yergin, *Shattered Peace*, p. 11; Dallin and Lapidus, "Reagan and the Russians," p. 206; Schneider, "Conservatism, Not Interventionism," p. 49; Zimmerman, "Rethinking Soviet Foreign Policy," p. 551. See also the definition of a "multipolar system" in K.J. Holsti, *International Politics: A Framework for Analysis* (Englewood Cliffs, NJ: Prentice-Hall, 1977), pp. 99-100. The term "accommodationist" is used by Michael A. Maggisto and Eugene R. Wittkoff, "American Public Attitudes Toward Foreign Policy," *International Studies Quarterly* 25 (December 1971), p. 611.

2 John A. Marcum, "Lessons of Angola," *Foreign Affairs* 54 (April 1976), p. 418; Ben-Zvi, "In Pursuit of National Security," p. 389; Sandler, "Linkage and Decoupling," p. 155; Gordon A. Craig and Alexander L. George, *Force and Statecraft: Diplomatic Problems of Our Time* (New York: Oxford University Press, 1983), p. 138.

3 Holsti, *International Politics*, p. 100.

4 J. Martin Rochester, "The Paradigm Debate in International Relations and its Implications for Foreign Policy Making: Towards a Redefinition of the National Interest," *Western Political Quarterly* XXXI (1978), p. 49; see also pp. 48-58 *passim;* George F. Kennan, *The Cloud of Danger* (Boston: Houghton Mifflin, 1977), pp. 228-234; Wolfgang Friedman, "Interventionism, Liberalism, and Power Politics: The Unfinished Revolution in International Thinking," *Political Science Quarterly* 83 (June 1968), p. 174; Seyom Brown, *The Faces of Power: Constancy and Change in United States Foreign Policy from Truman to Johnson* (New York: Columbia University Press, 1978), pp. 18-19; Roskin, "From Pearl Harbor to Vietnam," p. 576; Michael Nacht, "On Memories, Interests and Foreign Policy: The Case of Vietnam," in *Images and Reality in International Politics*, p. 188.

5 Holsti, "The Three-Headed Eagle," p. 351.

6   Hoffmann, *Dead Ends*, p. 91. See also Robert Legvold, "The Super Rivals: Conflict in the Third World," *Foreign Affairs* 57 (Spring 1979), p. 756.

7   Hoffmann, *Dead Ends*, p. 68. See also George, "Crisis Prevention Reexamined," p. 388; Lincoln P. Bloomfield, "United States Foreign Policy for the Mid-'80s: A New Grand Debate?" *International Journal* XXXVIII (Winter 1982/83), pp. 27.

8   Statement of Vice President Mondale, June 17, 1977, *Bulletin* LXXVII, p. 41. See also Seyom Brown, "An End to Grand Strategy," *Foreign Policy*, no. 32 (Fall 1978), p. 23; Novik, *Encounter with Reality*, pp. 7-8; John H. Herz, "Political Realism Revisited," *International Studies Quarterly* 25 (June 1981), pp. 192-196.

9   Cyrus Vance, *Hard Choices: Critical Years in America's Foreign Policy* (New York: Simon and Schuster, 1983), p. 27. See also Address by President Carter at Notre Dame University, May 22, 1977, in *Public Papers of the Presidents of the United States: Jimmy Carter, 1977*, Book I (Washington: US Government Printing Office, 1977), pp. 956-957. Parts of this address are reprinted in Appendix VI.

10   Address by Marshall D. Shulman, Special Adviser to the Secretary of State on Soviet Affairs, October 4, 1979, *Bulletin* LXXX, pp. 17-18. See also Richard J. Barnet, "US-Soviet Relations: The Need for a Comprehensive Approach," *Foreign Affairs* 57 (Spring 1979), p. 794; Garthoff, *Detente and Confrontation*, p. 565; Litwak, *Detente and the Nixon Doctrine*, p. 198.

11   Steven L. Spiegel, "Does the United States Have Options in the Middle East," *Orbis* 24 (Summer 1980), pp. 397-401. See also *idem, The Other Arab-Israeli Conflict*, p. 318; Ben-Zvi, "In Pursuit of National Security," p. 408; Huntington, "Renewed Hostility," p. 287; Novik, *Encounter with Reality*, pp. 7-8.

12   Spiegel, *The Other Arab-Israeli Conflict*, p. 318.

13   Kissinger, *Years of Upheaval*, p. 429. See also John C. Campbell, "The Middle East: The Burdens of Empire," *Foreign Affairs* 57 (Winter 1979), p. 616.

14   National Security Adviser Brzezinski interviewed on CBS Television, "Face the Nation," October 30, 1977, *Bulletin* LXXVII, p. 803.

15   Kissinger, *Years of Upheaval*, p. 755.

16   White House Statement, August 14, 1977, *Bulletin* LXXVII, p. 355.

17   President Carter's News Conference of June 30, 1977, *ibid.*, p. 147. See also Spiegel, *The Other Arab-Israeli Conflict*, p. 322.

18   Adviser Brzezinski interviewed on "Face the Nation," October 30, 1977, *Bulletin* LXXVII, p. 803. See also William B. Quandt, *Camp David: Peacemaking and Politics* (Washington, DC: The Brookings Institution, 1986), p. 119.

19   Statement of Secretary Kissinger of September 19, 1974, p. 508.

20   Seabury, "Reinspecting Containment," p. 45. See also Leslie Gelb, "The Kissinger Legacy," *New York Times Magazine*, October 31, 1976; George, "Domestic Constraints or Regime Change," p. 254.

21   Statement of Secretary Kissinger, September 19, 1974, p. 508. See also Breslauer, "Why Detente Failed," p. 326.

22   Statement of Zbigniew Brzezinski of June 1976. Quoted in "Statements on the Middle East," *Middle East Review* 9 (Spring 1977), p. 75.

23   Vance's May 23 interview is quoted in *Ibid*, p. 73. On the October 1976 memorandum see Vance, *Hard Choices*, pp. 418-447, and Spiegel, *The Other Arab-Israeli Conflict*, p. 322. See also, in this connection, Zbigniew Brzezinski, Francois Duchene and Kiichi Saeki, "Peace in an International Framework," *Foreign Policy* 19 (Summer 1975), p. 13; Touval, *The Peace Brokers*, pp. 286-287; Reich, *The United States and Israel*, p. 53.

24   Spiegel, "Does the United States Have Options?" p. 398; *idem, The Other Arab-Israeli Conflict*, p. 332.

25   Robert O. Freedman, "Detente and US-Soviet Relations in the Middle East During the Nixon Years," in Della W. Sheldon, ed., *Dimensions of Detente* (New York: Praeger, 1978), pp. 279, 323. See also Dina R. Spechler, "The Soviet Union in the Middle East: Problems, Policies and Prospective Trends," in *The Limits to Power*, p. 338; Lukacs, *Documents on the Israeli-Palestinian Conflict*, p. 15.

26   Touval, *The Peace Brokers*, pp. 240, 286; Ben-Zvi, *Alliance Politics*, pp. 25-27; Richard H. Ullman, "After Rabat: Middle East Risks and American Roles," *Foreign Affairs* 53 (January 1975), p. 287; Quandt, *Camp David*, p. 60.

27   Quoted in Spiegel, *The Other Arab-Israeli Conflict*, p. 332.

28   *Ibid.*, p. 336; *Time*, August 8, 1977.

29   Brzezinski, *Power and Principle*, pp. 104-105; Spiegel, *The Other Arab-Israeli Conflict*, p. 335; Quandt, *Camp David*, p. 84.

30   Quandt *Camp David*, p. 102.

31   Vance, *Hard Choices*, pp. 188-189; Zbigniew Brzenizki, *Power and Principle: Memoirs of the National Security Adviser, 1977-1981* (London: Weidenfeld and Nicolson, 1983), p. 102; Ben-Zvi, *Alliance Politics*, p. 26; Quandt, *Camp David*, p. 60.

32   *Ibid.*, pp. 91-92; Touval, *The Peace Brokers*, p. 287.

33   Brzezinski, *Power and Principle*, pp. 104-105; *Bulletin* LXXVII, pp. 639-640.

34   Vance, *Hard Choices*, pp. 191-192. See also Raymond Cohen, "Israel and the Soviet-American Statement of October 1, 1977: The Limits of Patron-Client Influence," *Orbis* 22 (Fall 1978), p. 619; Garthoff, *Detente and Confrontation*, p. 580; Quandt, *Camp David*, p. 119.

35   Breslauer, "Why Detente Failed," p. 330.

36   George, "Detente: The Search for a 'Constructive' Relationship," p. 21.

37   Holbraad, "Condominium and Concert," p. 3.

38   Brzezinski, Duchene, Saeki, "Peace in an International Framework," pp. 10, 16.

39   Candidate Carter's interview in the *Chicago Daily News*, May 8, 1976. Quoted in Steven L. Spiegel, *The Carter Approach to the Arab-Israeli Dispute* (paper delivered at the Shiloah Colloquium on the Middle East and the United States, March 23, 1978, Tel-Aviv University), p. 22.

40   Theodore Draper, "How Not to Make Peace in the Middle East," *Commentary* 67 (March 1979), p. 30.

41   Statement of President Carter, September 16, 1977. Quoted in *ibid.*, p. 29.

42   Statement by Adviser Brzezinski, October 18, 1977. Quoted in *ibid*. See also Jimmy Carter, *Keeping Faith: Memoirs of a President* (NY: Bantam Books, 1982), p. 293.

43   *Time*, August 8, 1977. Emphasis added. See also Ben-Zvi, *Alliance Politics*, p. 28.

44   Joint US-Soviet Statement on the Middle East, October 1, 1977, *Bulletin* LXXVII, pp. 639-640. Italics added. For the full text of the document see Appendix VII below.

45   Cohen, "Israel and the Soviet-American Statement," p. 626. See also Robert O. Freedman, "Soviet Policy in the Middle East: From the Sinai II Accord to the Egyptian-Israeli Peace Agreement," in W. Raymond Duncan, ed., *Soviet Policy in the Third World* (New York: Pergamon Press, 1980), p. 168.

46   Spiegel, *The Other Arab-Israeli Conflict*, p. 338. Emphasis original.

47   Sheehan, *The Arabs, Israelis, and Kissinger*, p. 257; Cohen, "Israel and the Soviet-American Statement," pp. 623, 626.

48   Cohen, "Israel and the Soviet-American Statement," p. 628.

49   Secretary Vance's News Conference of November 2, 1977, *Bulletin* LXXVII, p. 714. See also Abraham Ben-Zvi, "Soviet-American Relations: The Change from 1977 to 1980," *Middle East Focus* 3 (July 1980), p. 7.

50   Statement of Acting Prime Minister Ehrlich, October 2, 1977. Quoted in *The Jerusalem Post*, October 3, 1977. See also Cohen, "Israel and the Soviet-American Statement," p. 623.

51   *The Jerusalem Post*, October 3, 1977. See also Cohen, "Israel and the Soviet-American Statement," p. 623.

52   Ben-Zvi, *Alliance Politics*, p. 29. See also Wallace J. Thies, *When Governments Collide* (Berkeley: University of California Press, 1980), p. 282; and Reich, *The United States and Israel*, p. 54.

53   Alexander L. George, "The Development of Doctrine and Strategy," in *idem*, David K. Hall and William E. Simons, *The Limits of Coercive Diplomacy: Laos, Cuba, Vietnam* (Boston: Little, Brown, 1971), p. 27. See also Robert O. Keohane, "The Big Influence of Small Allies," *Foreign Policy* 2 (Spring 1971), p. 162; Yaacov Bar-Siman Tov, "Alliance Strategy: US-Small Allies Relationships," *The Journal of Strategic Studies* 3 (1980), pp. 202-203; David A. Baldwin, "Power Analysis and World Politics: New Trends Versus Old Tendencies," *World Politics* XXXI (January 1979), pp. 164, 166-167.

54   Israeli Foreign Minister Dayan interviewed in *Newsweek*, October 17, 1977. See also Cohen, "Israel and the Soviet-American Statement," pp. 631-632.

55   Tucker, "How Not to Make Peace," p. 30; Spiegel, "The United States and the Arab-Israeli Dispute," p. 354.

56   Harvey Sicherman, *Broker or Advocate? The US Role in the Arab-Israeli Dispute, 1973-1978* (Philadelphia: Foreign Policy Research Institute, 1978), p. 59. See also Spiegel, *The Other Arab-Israeli Conflict*, pp. 338-339.

57   George, "Domestic Constraints on Regime Change," p. 235.

58   *Ibid.*

59   Senator Henry Jackson interviewed on NBC Television's "Meet the Press," October 2, 1977. Quoted in Sicherman, *Broker or Advocate?*, p. 59. See also Ben-Zvi, *Alliance Politics*, p. 30. This senatorial reaction was reminiscent of the letter submitted to President Ford on May 22, 1975, which was signed by 76 senators and called upon the administration to support Israel politically, economically, and militarily.

60   Cohen, "Israel and the Soviet-American Statement," p. 624.

61   Spiegel, *The Other Arab-Israeli Conflict*, p. 338.

62   Sicherman, *Broker or Advocate?*, p. 59. See also Tillman, *The United States in the Middle East*, p. 234.

63   Ben-Zvi, *Alliance Politics*, p. 31.

64   *Ibid.* See also Tillman, *The United States in the Middle East*, p. 236.

65   Freedman, *Soviet Policy Toward the Middle East*, pp. 320-323. See also Garthoff, *Detente and Confrontation*, p. 582.

66   Nimrod Novik, *On the Shores of Bab Al-Mandab: Soviet Diplomacy and Regional Dynamics* (Philadelphia: Foreign Policy Research Institute, 1979), p. 44; Garthoff, *Detente and Confrontation*, p. 638.

67   President Carter's News Conference, January 12, 1978, *Weekly Compilation* 14 (1978), pp. 56-57. See also Garthoff, *Detente and Confrontation*, p. 591.

68   President Carter's News Conference, March 24, 1978, *Bulletin* LXXVIII, p. 26.

69 Statement by President Carter, May 12, 1978, *Weekly Compilation of Presidential Documents* 14 (1978), p. 903. See also address by President Carter, June 7, 1978, *Presidential Documents* 14, p. 1057.
70 Novik, *On the Shores of Bab Al-Mandab*, pp. 48-49.
71 Huntington, "Renewed Hostility," p. 278.
72 *Ibid.* For an analysis of the term: "operational environment" see Brecher, *The Foreign Policy System of Israel*, p. 11.
73 Garthoff, *Detente and Confrontation*, p. 652; see also p. 1077.
74 Stein, "The Alchemy of Peacemaking," p. 550.
75 *Ibid.*, pp. 550-551.
76 Spiegel, *The Other Arab-Israeli Conflict*, p. 372.
77 Quoted in *The Jerusalem Post*, October 6, 1978. See also Cohen, *International Relations*, p. 150; Huntington, "Renewed Hostility," pp. 282-283; Ben-Zvi, "In Pursuit of National Security," p. 409; Gaddis, *Strategies of Containment*, p. 348.
78 Strobe Talbott, "U.S.-Soviet Relations: From Bad to Worse," *Foreign Affairs: America and the World, 1972* 58 (1980), pp. 518, 522-523.
79 Garthoff, *Detente and Confrontation*, p. 946.
80 Brzezinski, *Power and Principle*, p. 429.
81 Quoted in Garthoff, *Detente and Confrontation*, p. 950.
82 Talbott, "U.S.-Soviet Relations," pp. 522-523.
83 Huntington, "Renewed Hostility," pp. 283-284. See also Spiegel, "Does the United States Have Options?" p. 403; Cohen, *International Politics*, pp. 150-153.
84 Bruce Russett and Donald R. Deluca, "'Don't Tread on Me': Public Opinion and Foreign Policy in the Eighties," Political Science Quarterly 96 (Fall 1981), p. 382.
85 *Ibid.*, pp. 382-383. See also Alvin Z. Rubinstein, "Soviet Policy in the Middle East: Perspectives from Three Capitals," in Robert H. Donaldson, ed., *The Soviet Union in the Third World: Successes and Failures* (Boulder: Westview Press, 1981), p. 152.
86 Garthoff, *Detente and Confrontation*, p. 958.
87 Address by Matthew Nimetz, Under-Secretary of State for Security Assistance, Science, and Technology, February 26, 1980, *Bulletin* LXXX, p. 33. See also Gaddis, "Containment," p. 18.
88 President Carter's remarks to members of Congress, January 8, 1980. Quoted in Garthoff, *Detente and Confrontation*, p. 972. Italics added.
89 *Ibid.*, p. 967.

Chapter 4

1 Breslauer, "Why Detente Failed," p. 230.
2 Glenn H. Snyder, "The Security Dilemma in Alliance Politics," *World Politics* XXXVI (July 1984), p. 486. See also Snyder and Diesing, *Conflict Among Nations*, p. 446.
3 Stein, "The Alchemy of Peacemaking," p. 552. See also Abraham Ben-Zvi, "In Pursuit of Peace in the Middle East: A Juxtaposition of American Strategies, 1969-79," *The Australian Journal of Politics and History* 27 (Winter 1981), p. 173.
4 Holsti, "Foreign Policy Formation Viewed Cognitively," p. 33.
5 Huntington, "Renewed Hostility," pp. 281-285.

6   Secretary Schultz's News Conference, May 31, 1985, *Official Text*, May 31, 1985.

7   Spiegel, *The Other Arab-Israeli Conflict*, p. 310. See also Address by Secretary Kissinger on September 16, 1975, *Bulletin* LXXIII, p. 499.

8   George, "Domestic Constraints on Regime Change," pp. 232-235.

9   I.M. Destler, "Congress," in *The Making of America's Soviet Policy*, pp. 54-55. Emphasis original. See also Snyder and Diesing, *Conflict Among Nations, p. 363.*

10   Breslauer, "Soviet Policy in the Middle East," p. 86. See also Atherton, "The Soviet Role in the Middle East," p. 709.

11   Vital, *The Survival of Small States*, pp. 84-85.

12   Oded Eran, "Soviet Middle East Policy, 1967-1973," in Itamar Rabinovich and Haim Shaked, eds., *From June to October: The Middle East Between 1967 and 1973* (New Brunswick: Transaction Books, 1978), pp. 45-46. See also Breslauer, "Soviet Policy in the Middle East," p. 69; Spechler, "The Soviet Union in the Middle East," p. 337; Golan, *Yom Kippur and After*, pp. 19, 246-247; Coit D. Blacker, "The Kremlin and Detente: Soviet Conceptions, Hopes, and Expectations," in *Managing US-Soviet Rivalry*, pp. 125-126.

13   Schneider, "Conservatism, Not Interventionism," pp. 39, 60.

14   Breslauer, "Soviet Policy in the Middle East, 1967-1972," p. 75. See also Tillman, *The United States in the Middle East*, p. 253.

15   Nimrod Novik, *The United States and Israel: Domestic Determinants of a Changing U.S. Commitment* (Boulder: Westview Press, 1986), pp. 34-35. See also Schneider, "Public Opinion," p. 33.

16   Novik, *The US and Israel*, p. 35; Ben-Zvi, *Alliance Politics*, pp. 9, 30; Schneider, "Public Opinion," p. 33.

17   Novik, *The US and Israel,* pp. 32, 35.

18   Reich, *The United States and Israel*, pp. 185-186.

19   Safran, *Israel: The Embattled Ally* (Cambridge, Mass: Harvard University Press, 1978), p. 572.

20   Robert H. True, *Interest Groups and the Foreign Policy Process: US Policy in the Middle East* (Beverly Hills: Sage Publications, 1976), pp. 56-57.

21   Reich, *Quest for Peace*, p. 374; Novik, *The US and Israel*, pp. 38-42.

22   Quandt, *Decade of Decision*, p. 22. See also Shoemaker and Spanier, *Patron-Client State Relationships*, p. 12.

23   B. Thomas Trout, "Rhetoric Revisited: Political Legitimation and the Cold War," *International Studies Quarterly* 19 (September 1975), p. 255. See also Davis B. Bobrow, "The Perspective of Great Power Foreign Policies: Steps in Context," in Jeffrey Z. Rubin, ed., *Dynamics of Third Party Intervention: Kissinger in the Middle East* (New York: Praeger 1981), p. 192.

24   George, "The Development of Doctrine and Strategy," pp. 26-27; Robert Jervis, "Deterrence Theory Revisited," *World Politics* XXXII (January 1979), p. 294; Richard Ned Lebow, "Misconceptions in American Strategic Assessment," *Political Science Quarterly* 97 (Summer 1982), p. 196; Ole R. Holsti, "Theories of Crisis Decision-Making," in Paul Gordon Lauren, ed., *Diplomacy: New Approaches in History, Theory, and Policy* (New York: The Free Press, 1979), p. 145; Chase, *A World Elsewhere*, p. 42; I.F. Stone, "The New Shape of Nixon's World," *The New York Review of Books*, June 29, 1972, p. 12; Robert Jervis, "Introduction: Approach and Assumptions," in Robert Jervis, Richard Ned Lebow and Janice Gross Stein, eds., *Psychology and Deterrence* (Baltimore: Johns Hopkins University Press, 1985), p. 3.

25   George, "The Development of Doctrine and Strategy," pp. 26-27. See also

Snyder and Diesing, *Conflict Among Nations*, p. 244; Thies, *When Governments Collide*, p. 244; Lebow, "Misconceptions in American Strategic Assessment," pp. 195-196; Bruce R. Kuniholm, "Carrots or Sticks? The Question of United States Influence over Israel," *International Journal* XXXVIII (Augumn 1983), p. 704.
26 Stein, "The Alchemy of Peacemaking," p. 543. See also Bar-Siman Tov, "Alliance Strategy," pp. 206-208; Ben-Zvi, *Alliance Politics*, p. 9.
27 Vital, *The Survival of Small States*, p. 124; Robert L. Rothstein, *The Weak in the World of the Strong* (New York: Columbia University Press, 1977), pp. 119-247; Keohane, "The Big Infuence," p. 162; Bar-Siman Tov, "Alliance Strategy," pp. 202-203; Michael I. Handel, "Does the Dog Wag the Tail or Vice Versa? Patron-Client Relations," *The Jerusalem Journal of International Relations* 6 (1982), pp. 28-29.
28 Janice Gross Stein, "Proxy Wars — How Superpowers End Them: The Diplomacy of War Termination in the Middle East," *International Journal* XXXV (Summer 1980), p. 496. See also Shoemaker and Spanier, *Patron-Client State Relationships*, pp. 12, 33-34; Vital, *The Survival of Small States*, p. 124; Michael I. Handel, *Weak States in the International System* (London: Frank Cass, 1981), pp. 190-195; Ben-Zvi, *Alliance Politics*, p. 8; Rubinstein, *Red Star on the Nile*, p. 334; Keith A. Dunn, "Soviet Involvement in the Third World: Implications of US Policy Assumption," in *The Soviets in the Third World*, pp. 422-423; Jon D. Glassman, *Arms for the Arabs* (Baltimore: Johns Hopkins University Press, 1975), p. 94; Tillman, *The United States in the Middle East*, pp. 250-257; Mangold, *Superpower Intervention in the Middle East*, p. 168; Garthoff, *Detente and Confrontation*, p. 361.
29 George, "The Arab-Israeli War of October 1973," p. 144; Golan, *Yom Kippur and After*, p. 23; Mohamed Heikal, *The Road to Ramadan* (London: Collins, 1975), p. 174; Atherton, "The Soviet Role in the Middle East," p. 699.
30 Kissinger, *White House Years*, p. 247; Sella, *Soviet Political and Military Conduct*, p. 74; Atherton, "The Soviet Role in the Middle East," p. 699; Garthoff, *Detente and Confrontation*, p. 315.
31 Rubinstein, *Red Star on the Nile*, p. 184. See also Shoemaker and Spanier, *Patron-Client State Relationships*, pp. 110-111; Anwar Sadat, *In Search of Identity* (New York: Harper & Row, 1978), p. 229; George, "The Arab-Israeli War of October 1973," p. 144; Golan, "The Arab-Israeli Conflict," p. 11. Marvin and Bernard Kalb, *Kissinger* (Boston: Little, Brown, 1974), pp. 450-451; Quandt, *Decade of Decisions*, p. 151; Kissinger, *Years of Upheaval*, p. 296; Hoffmann, "Detente," p. 241; Dawisha, *Soviet Foreign Policy Towards Egypt*, p. 63; Breslauer, "Soviet Policy in the Middle East, 1967-1982," p. 95.
32 Heikal, *The Road to Ramadan*, p. 174. See also Shoemaker and Spanier, *Patron-Client State Relationships*, p. 111.
33 Quoted in Raphael Israeli, *The Public Diary of President Sadat, Part I: The Road to War, October 1970-October 1973* (Leiden: E.J. Brill, 1978), p. 221. See also Heikal, *The Road to Ramadan*, pp. 174-175; Garthoff, *Detente and Confrontation*, pp. 315-316; William B. Quandt, "Soviet Policy in the October Middle East War-I," *International Affairs* 53 (July 1977), p. 379.
34 Quoted in Reich, *Quest for Peace*, pp. 203-204.
35 *Ibid.*, p. 204.
36 Heikal, *The Road to Ramadan*, p. 205. See also Atherton, "The Soviet Role in the Middle East," p. 699.
37 Quoted in Israeli, *The Public Diary of President Sadat*, Vol. I, p. 409.

38   Carter, *Keeping Faith*, p. 294. See also Janice Gross Stein, "Structures, Strategies, and Tactics of Mediation: Kissinger and Carter in the Middle East," *Negotiation Journal* 1 (October 1985), p. 336; Garthoff, *Detente and Confrontation*, p. 581; Quandt, *Camp David*, pp. 61-126; Ismail Fahmy, *Negotiations for Peace in the Middle East* (Baltimore: Johns Hopkins University Press, 1983), p. 236.

39   Vital, *The Survival of Small States*, p. 94. See also Ole R. Holsti, "Alliance and Coalition Diplomacy," in James N. Rosenau, Kenneth W. Thompson, and Gavin Boyd, eds., *World Politics: An Introduction* (New York: The Free Press, 1976), p. 350; Shahram Chubin, "Soviet-American Rivalry in the Middle East: The Political Dimension," in Adeed Dawisha and Karen Dawisha, eds., *The Soviet Union in the Middle East: Policies and Perspectives* (New York: Holmes & Meier, 1982), p. 132.

40   Russett and DeLuca, "Public Opinion and Foreign Policy." See also Schneider, "Conservatism, Not Interventionism," p. 34.

41   Daniel Yankelovich and John Doble, "The Public Mood: Nuclear Weapons and the USSR," *Foreign Affairs* 62 (Fall 1984), pp. 35-36. See also Schneider, "Conservatism, Not Interventiosnim," p. 34; *idem*, "Public Opinion," in *The Making of America's Soviet Policy*, p. 21.

42   Schneider, "Public Opinion," pp. 24-25. See also John E. Rielly, "American Opinion: Continuity, Not Reaganism," *Foreign Policy*, no. 50 (Spring 1983), p. 96.

43   Schneider, "Conservatism, Not Inteventionism," pp. 41-43.

44   *Ibid.*, pp. 41-43.

45   Holsti, "The Three-Headed Eagle," pp. 348-352.

46   For an early analysis of this possibility, see Vital, *The Survival of Small States*, p. 95.

47   George, "Crisis Prevention Reexamined," p. 377; Cohen, *International Relations*, p. 52; Evron, "Great Powers Military Intervention," p. 22.

48   Cohen, *International Relations*, p. 52.

49   For an analysis which underscores the role of the local disputants in mitigating the Arab-Israeli predicament see Vital, *The Survival of Small States*, p. 96.

The Jaffee Center for Strategic Studies (JCSS)

The Center for Strategic Studies was established at Tel-Aviv University at the end of 1977. In 1983 it was named the Jaffee Center for Strategic Studies in honor of Mr. and Mrs. Mel Jaffee. The objective of the Center is to contribute to the expansion of knowledge on strategic subjects and to promote public understanding of and pluralistic thought on matters of national and international security.

The Center relates to the concept of strategy in its broadest meaning, namely, the complex of processes involved in the identification, mobilization and application of resources in peace and war, in order to solidify and strengthen national and international security.

INTERNATIONAL BOARD OF TRUSTEES

JCSS Publications

JCSS publications present the findings and assessments of the Center's research staff. Each paper represents the work of a single investigator or a team. Such teams may also include research fellows who are not members of the Center's staff. Views expressed in the Center's publications are those of the authors and do not necessarily reflect the views of the Center, its trustees, officers, or other staff members or the organizations and individuals that support its research. Thus the publication of a work by JCSS signifies that it is deemed worthy of public consideration but does not imply endorsement of conclusions or recommendations.

The Jaffee Center for Strategic Studies Recent Publications in English

1985 Subscription Series

Study no. 1   Nimrod Novik, *Encounter with Reality: Reagan and the Middle East During the First Term.*

Study no. 2   Anat Kurz and Ariel Merari, *ASALA: Irrational Terror or Political Tool.*

Study no. 3   Efraim Karsh, *The Cautious Bear: Soviet Military Engagement in Middle East Wars in the Post 1967 Era.*

Study no. 4   Shemuel Meir, *Strategic Implications of the New Oil Reality.*

1986 Subscription Series

Study no. 5   Abraham Ben-Zvi, *The American Approach to Superpower Collaboration in the Middle East, 1973-1986.*

Study no. 6   Ariel Merari and Shlomi Elad, *The International Dimension of Palestinian Terrorism.*

Study no. 7   Saul Cohen, *The Geopolitics of Israel's Border Question.*

Study no. 8   Yehuda Ben-Meir, *National Security Decisionmaking: The Israeli Case.*

Books

Shai Feldman, *Israeli Nuclear Deterrence: A Strategy for the 1980s* (New York: Columbia University Press, 1983).

Mark Heller, *A Palestinian State: The Implications for Israel* (Cambridge: Harvard University Press, 1983).

Zvi Lanir, ed., *Israeli Security Planning in the 1980s* (New York: Praeger, 1984).

Aryeh Shalev, *The West Bank: Line of Defense* (New York: Praeger, 1985).

Ariel Merari, ed., *Terrorism and Counter-Terrorism* (Frederick, Md: UPA, 1985).

Nimrod Novik, *The United States and Israel: Domestic Determinants of a Changing US Commitment* (Boulder: Westview, 1986).

Annuals

The Middle East Military Balance, published since 1983 for JCSS by The Jerusalem Post and Westview Press.

InTer, A Review of International Terrorism.

83   91